Software Process Improvement
With CMM

For a complete listing of the *Artech House Computer Science Library*,
turn to the back of this book.

Software Process Improvement With CMM

Joseph Raynus

Artech House
Boston • London

Library of Congress Cataloging-in-Publication Data
Raynus, Joseph.
   Software process improvement with CMM / Joseph Raynus.
      p.   cm. — (Artech House computer science library)
   Includes bibliographical references and index.
   ISBN 0-89006-644-2 (alk. paper)
    1. Computer software—development.   2. Capability maturity model
(Computer software).   I. Title.   II. Series.
   QA76.76.D47R3873   1998
   005.1—dc21   98-44785
                                                            CIP

British Library Cataloguing in Publication Data
Raynus, Joseph
   Software process improvement with CMM
   1. Software reengineering   2. Software productivity   3. Software maintenance
   I. Title
   005.1'6

   ISBN 0-89006-644-2

Cover design by Lynda Fishbourne

© 1999 ARTECH HOUSE, INC.
685 Canton Street
Norwood, MA 02062

International Standard Book Number: 0-89006-644-2
Library of Congress Catalog Card Number: 98-44785

10 9 8 7 6 5 4 3 2

To my wife Gail,
who made it happen.

Contents

Foreword

O ccasionally during our lives, we get an opportunity to meet a unique individual or to discover a product that changes our reference point with regard to how we feel about certain things. For me, the individual was Joe Raynus, and the product was one of his implementations of software engineering metrics. I met him in the late 1980s after hearing about an unbelievable product he was developing that would automate the generation of software metrics and assist in the analysis of the results. Needless to say, after weeks of discussions and evaluations, I understood not only the product and how it worked but the man behind the product and how he thought. In a nutshell, he was able to take very complex processes and calculations and reduce them to management terms and graphs that I could easily understand and communicate. While many software experts were still discussing software engineering as an art, Joe was explaining to product managers how to relate what they previously understood to the discipline of software engineering.

While much of Joe's work was evolving, so was the knowledge that was being collected and documented at Carnegie Mellon's Software Engineering Institute (SEI). While many of us who worked in and around defense software programs remember that SEI's Capability Maturity Model was created to assist government program managers to better understand the maturity of a company bidding on government work, we forget that much of the content was based on understanding how and why failures occur in software development activities. As I compare the problems I faced in the government sector with the issues and concerns my peers and I now face in the commercial shrink-wrap marketplace, I realize the problems are the same. Speed, quality, requirements satisfaction, test methods, configuration management, program planning and oversight, cost, risk management, and predictability keep coming up, whether in a small startup or a large government software developer.

SEI's knowledge and Joe's wisdom are captured in the forthcoming pages that will assist any software company to become a better producer of world-class products. His approach is simple and straightforward, his examples are clear, and his practical experience "spot on." I would encourage all my peers in the commercial sector who are confronted with the challenges of leading software improvement activities in their organizations to look closely at CMM and Joe's work to help you with the journey. And, if you don't know yet, many of your competitors are already implementing the key processes that will give them cycle time and quality advantages you wish you had today.

Michael J. Prowse
Director, Quality and Customer Loyalty
Solaris Software, Sun Microsystems, Inc.

Preface

Fifteen years ago my boss's boss called me into his office and fired at me three "simple" questions:

1. "Why is it so expensive to support and maintain our software products?"
2. "What is the reliability of our product?"
3. "What is the average cost of one software bug?"

The answers to these questions became a beginning for me. That was when I became a troubleshooter and troublemaker. A few years later I started a company, in which the main product was the automated software metrics tool.

I was a manager and software vendor then. Sometimes in life, a person will need to make difficult decisions. I left the company that I founded and a product that was very dear to me and went back into industry. I saw my mission as helping my clients answer the same questions my boss asked me.

Very soon, I realized that in order to understand the problem, you have to "go to the trenches and talk to the troops." It is impossible to provide a prepackaged solution to the problem, even if it is a set of software metrics. Each client's case is unique, and until you are able to understand a particular problem, you cannot advise.

There is no organization like the U.S. Air Force for understanding the problem of software management. For almost a year I was a technical advisor to the Source Selection Evaluation Board (SSEB). Reviewing different proposals I got a good grasp of how the potential problems look from the outside, how ugly they can be, what is expected, and how volatile the process of software acquisition can be.

I was a customer then. After the SSEB, I spent a few more years helping my customers manage and keep their software problems under control. I taught a lot and traveled a lot (and still do). I was putting the pieces of the software development puzzle together for my clients. Sometimes, the obvious information was hidden from their view. I have lived their lives and helped them solve their problems.

Then I became a consultant. My introduction to the Capability Maturity Model (CMM) was very important to me. The number of assessments conducted (I was part of the evaluation team) helped me to understand the full depth of the software management problems. At the same time, I understood that the methodology was available to help us navigate the Everglades of software project management. The freedom of navigation comes through the flexibility of the interpretation.

My interpretation comes from the following very simple point of view: Do what is right and practical for the software industry so it can become better and more mature.

I started to use CMM as a reference guide and software metrics as a foundation and glue for the software process improvement effort. I introduced this methodology to my customers. They used it and they helped me to improve on it.

I've learned that the best approach to any task is to do what makes sense for you!

Note to the reader

Throughout the book, I use Sufi stories about the wise fool Mulla Nasrudin. The Sufis believe that intuition is the only real guide to knowledge and use these stories as exercises. The stories can be applied to many different situations, including the software management process. The source for the Sufi stories is Indries Shah's *The Pleasantries of the Incredible Mulla Nasrudin* (ARKANA Penguin Books, reprint edition 1993).

> *"What is Fate?" Nasrudin was asked by a scholar.*
> *"An endless succession of intertwined events, each influencing the other."*
> *"That is hardly a satisfactory answer. I believe in cause and effect."*
> *"Very well," said Nasrudin, "look at that." He pointed to a procession passing in the street. "That man is being taken to be hanged. Is that because someone gave him a silver piece and enabled him to buy the knife with which he committed the murder or because someone saw him do it or because nobody stopped him?"*

Acknowledgments

I thank the following people and organizations for their support during the writing of this book:

The U.S. Air Force for giving me an opportunity to work on major projects; Lt. General Stansberry (USAF Ret.) for his everlasting support and encouragement; Ron Radice for giving me a courage and convincing me to write this book; Larry Putnam for sharing information and supporting me in this venture; Bob Webster (USAF) for supporting my quest for common sense and metrics; Mike Prowse (SunSoft) for listening, talking, and sharing; Don Crittenden (USMC) and Cynthia Gregory (SunSoft) for always trying hard; Joe Morin from Integrated Systems Diagnostics for teaching me the CMM and allowing me to be part of his team; Brian Hermann for providing information for the case study; Jonathan Plant (Artech House) for walking me through the process of book publishing and not giving up on me on the way; my wonderful customers for solving their software management problems; and my remarkable family for their love, support, and patience. Special thanks to my son David, who helped me with the charts and graphs.

Thank you all very much.

Introduction

Today's problems come from yesterday's "solutions."

Peter Senge, *The Fifth Discipline*

Some of the follies we commit because of false maps in our heads are so commonplace that we do not think of them as remarkable.

S. I. Hayakawa, *Language in Thought and Action*

Outside of our everyday business endeavors, we are living very normal and logical lives. We have goals. One goal is usually that of finding a way to achieve stability and manage our lives. We make a commitment to ourselves and to our families to improve the quality of our being. We go to schools and train ourselves to be able to get better jobs and better financial rewards. We develop our ability to perform through education, goal orientation, and internal organization. We track our family activities through better planning and sometimes even learn from our past mistakes. We use measurements every day of our lives and make different important (or not very important) decisions based on them. The weather forecast for the next day is a good example: We might take extra time to get ready for work because of the possibility of rain or snow; we'll dress accordingly and may decide to take an umbrella.

On a daily basis, without even realizing it, our behavior involves a dynamically interrelated set of activities. In the course of 24 hours we spend about 7.5 hours sleeping, about 8.5 hours at work, 1.5 hours in traffic, 1.4 hours in different activities, 1.1 hour in activities related to physical health, and so on. We do not measure our activities, but we can estimate and plan them well. The dynamics of those activities come naturally to us.

Finally, when we come to work every day, our logic disappears, and new life begins. In his book *Powers of Mind*, Adam Smith describes a Stanford experiment. A team of psychologists raised batches of kittens, some of whom were brought up seeing only vertical stripes and some of whom were brought up in a horizontally striped world. After they grew up and were allowed to move anywhere, the vertical stripers thought the world was vertical and the horizontal stripers thought the world was horizontal. The horizontal stripers could not see the vertical world, and vice versa. The psychologists wrote: "Functional neural connections can be selectively and predictably modified by environmental situation." In other words, *our experience shapes our perception.* We adapt to our environment without really understanding it.

What is our perception in relation to everyday work activities, particularly in managing large software-intensive projects? With large projects, resources leak as if through a giant sieve.

I have been an observer and active participant in the software development business for the last eighteen years. As a manager and software process improvement consultant, I have spent a significant amount of time in many software development organizations, talking with senior management as well as software developers in the United States, Europe, Japan, and Australia.

Unfortunately, what I have seen has not been very encouraging. With the exception of very few companies, software development organizations do not respond well to the process improvement innovations related to software development. Fear surrounds the thought of trying something new; this fear is accentuated by constant pressure to produce the product on time and within budget.

Until recently, the vast majority of software companies did not view software development process management and improvement to be of strategic importance to the future of the company. Process improvement and its relationship to software quality, cost, and ability to meet schedules were never considered to be either useful weapons or, very often, differentiating factors against the competition.

Nonetheless, a well-managed software development process can be viewed as an iterative process of information exchange and allows software development organizations a clear view and understanding of available information, providing a foundation for analysis and management of the software process based on hard facts and not vague assumptions.

To be able to withstand the pressure of competition, to save money, and to improve the quality of production software, a progressive software development organization needs to realize the necessity for implementing and managing an efficient and effective software development process.

This book reviews the Capability Maturity Model (CMM) and examines multiple relationships between measurable process quantities and characteristics. I demonstrate different ways in which measurable elements can be linked and used to define and improve the behavior of a software development organization. Organizations will be able to design, build, and implement high-quality software products in spite of unexpected organizational and personnel changes, implementation of new technologies, or changes in customer requirements.

I hope this book will lead you to a better understanding of how measurements, common sense, and simple logic can help you to improve your software process and project management by using CMM as a guiding framework that provides a structure for software process improvement. Without this integrating structure, software process improvement is just a collection of conflicting data, unrelated practices, and sometimes meaningless procedures.

1

Software Management Process and CMM

The process of software development

Software development can be described as the process of producing a software product. This process has three main components: (1) the software developer, (2) the organization, and (3) the process of product development.

The software developer creates the product through hard work and dedication, by "burning the midnight oil." But do the software developers really know what they are creating and what the end result is supposed to look like? Will the product they create fit into the "big picture" of integrated products, and how will their code impact the rest of the product? They may be saying to themselves "I have no idea what the customer really wants," "No one asked me if it is possible to implement this," and

"I do not have the training, the tools, the proper resources, or the time to do this job right."

The organization, which supports the software developer, defines policies, goals, budgets, and performance measures. What does the organization do to achieve product quality? The organization is built around people, not around tasks. In a reactive organization, people are assigned to a project based on their availability—not their abilities, experience, or skill level.

The real reporting structure in software development organizations is sometimes not well defined. This leads to confusion, as reflected in the following, common statement: "I mostly report to X, but in some cases I report to Y; on a special project I report to Z." This statement does not reflect the flexibility of the organization. This statement reflects the lack of planning and the lack of policies and procedures describing how to accomplish a task and who is responsible for what.

The process of product development includes management of customer requirements, the design process, code development, integration, and testing. As an organization, ask yourself the following questions: Can you measure the quality of the process? How do you know how good your processes are? Can you identify the key process that affects customer quality? Is it customer requirements management? Is it software configuration management? Is it project management? If your management does not have answers to these questions, it means that your organization does not have any understanding of the role of quality in your organization.

Most of the time, there are plenty of process improvement opportunities in any organization, but they are often associated with problems. One of the most common opportunities is the opportunity to set up an organizational system to manage costs, scheduling, and quality. This organizational system will eventually become independent of any organizational changes and will help to improve organization, process, and individual developers' performance.

Well, now you've got the message. Let's try to figure out how to improve the process of software development and not lose track of what we do. The Capability Maturity Model (CMM) can provide such guidance and can be used successfully as a navigation tool for the software process improvement journey.

Software management and your organization

The scope of this book goes beyond a simple discussion of the different characteristics of CMM. CMM can be rigid, conceptualized, and flexible at the same time. As with any other model, the rigidity of it lies in the model's representation and its description. The flexibility of the model lies in its interpretation and implementation.

CMM is a conceptual model, but, at the same time, it has all of the necessary qualities of any other model. It is generalized; it represents major aspects of the software development process that are appropriate to the associated problems; and it has the capability (if used the right way) to define the behavior of the organization. CMM is intended to provide different levels of assurance that will help minimize the risk and the horror stories associated with the software development process.

Let's take a look at the Malcolm Baldrige National Quality Awards (MBNQA) for 1997. The criteria for the Baldrige awards are based on company performance in each of seven categories. The criteria require the award applicant to provide information on the company's improvement processes, results, and the effectiveness of the approach. Looking at the Baldrige award criteria (Table 1.1) is a good way to determine what should be fixed within a company. It enables management to look at the quality of internal processes and assess the goodness of process performance against the standards.

The CMM can be interpreted in a very similar manner and can provide an understanding of and also guide the process of software development.

CMM points out that the software product development cycle does not exist on its own and does not start with code production. It is part of the overall company strategy and includes the very diligent process of project planning, estimation, and management. Many organizations are beginning to realize that the software development process is no longer considered an art form. To be successful, it needs to become a science.

Some companies are doing defect prevention and requirements management, project cost estimation, and risk analysis. Some companies can quantify and produce charts and graphs on how well their development organization performed last year. But can they quantify how their

Table 1.1
Malcolm Baldrige National Quality Award Criteria

	Category	Point Value
1	Leadership	110
1.1	Leadership system	80
1.2	Company responsibility and citizenship	30
2	Strategic planning	80
2.1	Strategy development process	40
2.2	Company strategy	40
3	Customer and market focus	80
3.1	Customer and market knowledge	40
3.2	Customer satisfaction and relationship enhancement	40
4	Information and analysis	80
4.1	Selection and use of information and data	25
4.2	Selection and use of comparative information and data	15
4.3	Analysis and review of company performance	40
5	Human resource development and management	100
5.1	Work system	40
5.2	Employee education training and development	30
5.3	Employee well-being and satisfaction	30
6	Process management	100
6.1	Management of product and service processes	60
6.2	Management of support processes	20
6.3	Management of supplier and partnering processes	20
7	Business results	450
7.1	Customer satisfaction results	130
7.2	Financial and market results	130
7.3	Human resource results	35
7.4	Supplier and partner results	25
7.5	Company specific results	130
	Total points 1000	

development process measures up against the competition? By failing to understand the importance of implementing a continuous measurement and improvement process, they fall into a false sense of security.

What is the benefit of continuous process improvement? According to Dr. Joseph Juran, the quality expert of Deming's generation, the quality improvement should be 40% per year from the first year of implementation [1]. "Wait a second," you might say; that is what CMM Level 5 is supposed to be, and for many organizations this is an unreachable dream!

A few years ago, I came across some very interesting data published by Larry Putnam [2]. In this article Larry Putnam quotes Herb Krasner's research, which was done on software systems of approximately 500,000 software lines of code (SLOC). Let us analyze the information presented in Table 1.2. Looking at the cost column we can see that cost reduction from one level to another level is approximately 40%. This number corresponds to the findings of Dr. Juran very well. That is why we are going to talk about using the CMM structure as a guideline not only for project management but also for structuring improvements based on specific needs and resources.

What does successful and flexible CMM interpretation and implementation mean for your organization? It means process and business improvements:

- *What kinds of improvements in your business will it provide?* It will provide predictability, control, effectiveness, and competitiveness.

- *What is it going to improve?* It will improve the competitiveness of your organization.

Table 1.2

Research on Software Defects. (*Source:* Copyright 1990 Herb Krasner.)

Level	Quality (defects/KSLOC*)	Productivity	Cost (millions of dollars)	Development Time (months)
L1	9	1 SLOC/hr	32.5	40
L2	3 defects/KSLOC	3 SLOC/hr	15	32
L3	1 defect/KSLOC	5 SLOC/hr	6.5	25
L4	.3 defects/KSLOC	8 SLOC/hr	2.5	19
L5	.1 defects/KSLOC	12+ SLOC/hr	1	16

* KSLOC = 1,000 SLOC

- *What does it mean for your business?* It means a reduced bottom line and increased productivity.

At any organizational level, managers have to verify and control the progress of a software product development process. Do you have the means to control it? Most companies cannot control software development. They drive the process depending on luck and gut feelings.

A lot of folly results because of management's misunderstanding of processes and quantitative misrepresentations of the process they are managing.

One very respectable company, which has been in a software development business for many years, stated in one of its proposals to a customer: "Our software development process is so advanced that we can deliver more code in the same period of time than our customers required!"

We need a new way of looking at the software development process. It has been taken for granted for too long. The old way of developing and managing software is no longer adequate.

What are you waiting for?

Nasrudin's wife sent him to the river for water. She could not go, she explained, even though it was women's work, because she was waiting for the dough to rise. Nasrudin wandered to the riverside, reached in with the pot, and lost it in the water. An hour later he was still sitting there, looking steadily into the water. Someone passing by asked him what he was doing. "Waiting," he said, "for the dough to rise."

Obviously, Nasrudin had a long wait ahead. Are you waiting as futilely as Nasrudin to change your software development process? Can you afford to wait? Are you waiting for more excuses?

- "Process improvement just isn't going to work."
- "Process is bureaucracy."

- "Process means documenting. I am not going to document anything. It's too much work!"

- "This is going to stifle my creativity."

- "We are going to have to use a process that does not relate to what we do today."

- "Process is impractical in this job."

- "Process leaves out the people. Management thinks that if there is a process, then anybody can do the job. Our knowledge and experience become irrelevant."

- "This is *not* going to be forced on us."

What is really going on in the organization? Do you hear these types of comments?

- "I have no idea what the customer really wants."

- "The schedule keeps slipping."

- "No one asked me if it was possible to implement this!"

- "I did implement that requirement!"

- "I do not have the training, the tools, the proper resources, or the time to do this job right."

- "I am new here and I can't figure out where anything is."

- "All I do is fix bugs."

So what are the real problems then? Let us define the behavior pattern of such an organization.

- Reactive not proactive. (Projects are managed from crisis to crisis.)

- Few rules or policies. (Railroad engineer's philosophy: "Show me the tracks and get out.")

- No estimation or planning. (Everybody is way too busy.)

- People's responsibilities are not clearly defined. (Whose job is it?)

- Inconsistent performance. (There is no organizational memory established in terms of what works and what does not work.)

- No preplanning. (If it is not a problem, we don't have time for it.)

- Management responds only to crises. (There is no control over what the development organization does.)

- Customer commitment is constantly tested and changed. (Risk evaporates commitments.)

As a result, organizations end up with large costs and scheduling and quality problems because the lack of internal processes compromises product quality.

References

[1]   Juran, J., *Juran on Leadership in Quality*, NY: The Free Press, 1985.

[2]   Putnam, L., "Linking the QSM Productivity Index with the SEI Maturity Levels," QSM internal working document.

2

Capability Maturity Model

Organization of the CMM

The CMM developed by the Software Engineering Institute (SEI) has been explained in great detail in different publications. Some of you have probably already read about it, gone through CMM training, or been trained on how to conduct a software capability evaluation (SCE).

CMM is a conceptual framework that represents process management of software development. CMM contains five maturity levels or stages [1].

1. *Level 1, initial:* The software process is characterized as ad hoc, chaotic, and heroic. Few processes are defined or followed, and project success depends on individual effort. There is no formal management control over software development.

2. *Level 2, repeatable:* This level provides an introduction to the formal, documented process. Basic management processes are

9

established to control cost, scheduling, and functionality. The necessary process discipline is in place to repeat previous successes on projects with similar applications. Elevation from Level 1 to Level 2 means that the organization has established project management control, established a software engineering process group (SEPG), and formally introduced software engineering methods and techniques.

3. *Level 3, defined:* This level provides a foundation for continuous process improvement by establishing the necessary process management functions to control process parameters. The software process for both management and engineering activities is documented, standardized, and integrated into a standard software process for the organization. All projects use a tailored version of the organization's standard software process for developing and maintaining software.

4. *Level 4, managed:* Detailed measures of the software process and product quality are collected. Both the software process and products are quantitatively understood and controlled.

5. *Level 5, optimized:* Continuous process improvement is enabled by quantitative feedback from the process and from piloting innovative ideas and technologies.

These five maturity levels define an original scale for measuring the maturity of an organization's software process and for evaluating its software process capability (Figure 2.1). Each maturity level indicates the level of process capability.

Levels 2 through 5 are decomposed into 18 key process areas (KPAs) as shown in Figure 2.2. Each KPA is organized into five sections, called *common features*.

1. *Commitment to perform:* Describes the actions that must take place within the organization to ensure that the process is established and will function. The commitment to perform feature usually involves developing organizational policies and senior management sponsorship.

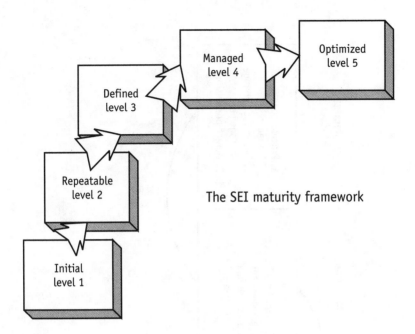

Figure 2.1   SEI maturity framework.

2. *Ability to perform:* Describes the preconditions that must exist in the project or organization to implement the software process competently. It usually includes resources, training, organizational structures, and tools.

3. *Activities performed:* Describes the roles and procedures necessary to implement a key process area. This feature typically involves establishing plans and procedures, performing the work, tracking it, and taking corrective actions as necessary.

4. *Measurement and analysis:* Describes the need to measure the process and analyze the measurements. The measurement and analysis feature typically includes examples of the measurements that could be taken to determine the status and effectiveness of the activities performed feature.

5. *Verifying implementation:* Describes the steps to ensure that the activities are performed in compliance with the process that has

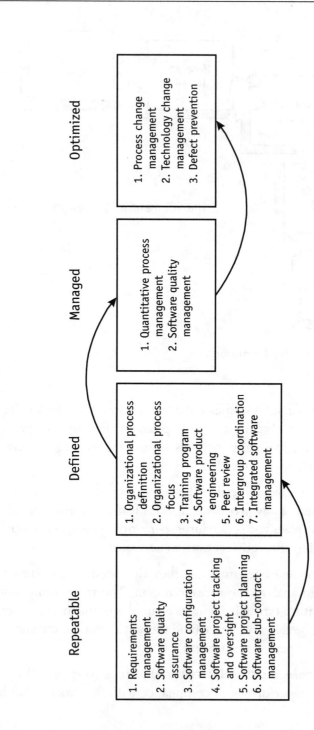

Figure 2.2   CMM levels and KPAs.

been established. Verifying typically means reviews and audits by management and software quality assurance.

The practices in the activity performed common feature (item 3 above) describe what must be implemented to establish a process capability.

Key practices (CMM has 316 suggested) describe the infrastructure and activities that contribute to the effective implementation and institutionalization of the key process area. The key practices describe "what" should be done, but do not mandate "how" it is to be done. They do not require a specific model of the software life cycle such as a waterfall or spiral. They do not demand a specific organizational structure. They do not judge a technical approach to product implementation or the development tools used. They merely suggest; that is, they do not mandate. Instead they leave the "how" up to each individual organization. The CMM is a management model. It gives you a guideline on how to manage a software process and does not judge the technical aspects of the product development or the performance of the developers.

The software process improvement and level achievements of the SEI CMM are very similar in nature and have the same objective: to improve how software is developed. Software process improvement is a general issue, the specifics of which are addressed in CMM. Three main issues are related to software process improvement and software project management: (1) cost, (2) scheduling, and (3) quality.

These issues often become big, pathological problems, which end up making the whole organization dysfunctional. These issues are not technical issues. These issues are issues of management—the issues of how to manage and identify the impact of present or potential problems. How do we prevent an issue from becoming a problem?

The *improvement* in the term *software process improvement* refers to an improvement in management techniques! That is what most companies had not realized earlier. This is where both the nature of conflict (us versus them) and inconsistency in organizational goals arise. "All too often, proactiveness is reactiveness in disguise. If we simply become more aggressive fighting the enemy out there, we are reacting—regardless of what we call it. True proactiveness comes from seeing how we contribute to our own problems. It is a product of our way of thinking, not our emotional state" [2].

I was told this story: Once upon a time, a big company invited a very famous consultant to its headquarters for a discussion about CMM and software process improvement. The company published a memorandum requiring the participation of all software managers in the meeting. The first thing the consultant said was that "the cause of poor quality is poor management." Right there, the management immediately lost any interest, and after the break, the room was almost empty. The company never invited the consultant back.

The five CMM levels

Now we take a look the five CMM levels in a little more detail.

Level 1: initial

The first question I ask new clients is this: "When was your last reorganization?" Why do I ask that question? Because I need a starting point.

Unfortunately, the initial level processes are the most practiced processes in the software business. Companies develop these processes over time and develop ownership. To some degree, they represent the reality of the software development organization: pressures, crises, and limitations. As the processes grow, more and more software developers get involved. A particular process can became so complex that nobody knows exactly how and why it works. The Level 1 processes constantly change, just as organizations change. Processes are not documented so people cannot really understand them. The success of Level 1 organizations in product development comes not from the project management function but from the efforts of individuals performing their specific tasks without a clear understanding how the process works. I like to compare the Level 1 organization with a typical John Wayne movie, in which the main character is a hero who always saves the new settlers from the bad guys.

One of the interesting characteristics of the Level 1 organization is that management's presence is very strong, but very inefficient due to the lack of communications. As a result, the quality and the delivery schedule of the product is unpredictable. At this point, the management and management decisions become very unpopular among the practitioners [3].

At Level 1, management's remedy to improve a process is to reorganize. They believe the process is okay, but the way in which management executes the process is wrong. In the first few months after a reorganization the productivity of the employees usually increases; fear drives them, fear of management. The productivity of the department increases not because the process has been improved by the reorganization, but because extra hours are spent at the terminal.

What is the next step to address symptoms not problems? Another reorganization!

Level 2: repeatable

At this level, basic project management processes are established to track costs, schedules, and functionality. The necessary process discipline is in place to repeat earlier successes on projects with similar applications [1].

A repeatable process is a documented process. The process should be communicated on all levels with the help of documented procedures. (By the way, if your organization does not have documented procedures, you failed the assessment.)

At Level 2 the project managers shift their attention from technical issues to organizational and managerial issues. Therefore, they should have two basic abilities: (1) the ability to determine and communicate the status of a project as accurately as possible and (2) the ability to estimate the impact of past decisions and document and review them in terms of scheduling, effort, and product quality.

You start your continuous process improvement at the repeatable level by listening to your software practitioners and by documenting the process with formal procedures. These procedures will be used across the organization and continuously improved. Everybody wants action—discussions take time. *Level 2 is about listening, communicating, and documenting* [3].

Level 2 is concerned primarily with how the organization estimates, defines, and determines the status of a project and with the impact of decisions in terms of costs, scheduling, and quality. The following issues are very important at the repeatable level:

- Impact of changed commitments to the customer;

- How the software requirements baseline has been modified, how extensive the changes are, and how changes are controlled and communicated;

- Impact of the work effort (how the resources are planned in order to implement the customer's requirements and allocated to accommodate the modifications);

- Impact of the schedule (how the schedule is modified based on changed commitments);

- Impact of costs (determining the cost implications of the modifications).

Because these project management issues are interdependent, CMM suggests ways to control the process and suggests the metrics approach for qualifying and quantifying the impact of modifications.

The repeatable process enables organizations to integrate the historical analysis of past performance into documented procedures to improve continually. With the use of measurement, a historical analysis of previous projects (procedures, interpretations, and knowledge base required) can take place, providing management with information about design, scheduling, quality, and costs. This information helps management make qualified decisions before contractual obligations are made. *Historical analysis is a technique that allows organizations to "adjust future conduct based on past performance."*

Historical analysis of previous projects is necessary to establish and understand the pattern of how the organization develops the product. Project history data fall into three major categories: software development, operational data, and maintenance data. *Software development data* and *operational data* describe the characteristics of the project (e.g., product, process, and resources) and form the foundation for developing estimation and prediction models. *Software maintenance data* describe the behavior of the product (e.g., its successes/failures and modifications history).

The approach is to determine systematically answers to the following questions when looking at historical analyses:

- What is known about the past project?

- What is unclear?

- What is assumed?

- In what ways are past project implementations similar?

- In what ways are past project implementations different?

Each question demands a factual answer, and these can only be obtained through analysis and investigation. If objective answers are obtained, then the decision is much less likely to be faulty.

Level 3: defined

The software process for both management and engineering activities is documented, standardized, and integrated into an organization-wide software process. All projects use a documented and approved version of the organization's process for developing and maintaining software [1].

Level 3 supports projects by institutionalizing and expanding the main principles of Level 2 across the entire organization. At Level 3 tasks are being formally defined and documented. Level 3 shifts the emphasis from the project itself to organizational support of the project. Level 3 is built on the project management foundation of Level 2. If the repeatable level defines what to do and who should do it, the defined level specifies when to do it and how to do it (Figure 2.3).

Level 3 establishes a common understanding of the process across the organization and also provides flexibility in terms of how to change

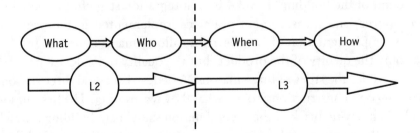

Figure 2.3 Transition from Level 2 to Level 3.

the process and relate it to ongoing activities. It provides the foundation for the quality of management decisions.

At maturity Level 3, the organization not only defines its process in terms of software engineering standards and methods, it also makes a series of organizational and methodological improvements. These improvements include design and code reviews, training programs for developers and review leaders, and increased organizational focus on software engineering. The establishment of a software engineering process group is considered to be one of the major improvement of this phase, and it focuses on the software engineering process and the adequacy with which it is implemented.

A process cannot be defined if we do not know *how* the process flows throughout the organization.

Level 4: managed

In Level 4, detailed measures of the software process and product quality are collected. Both the software process and products are quantitatively understood and controlled using detailed measures [1]. The KPAs of Level 4 are probably the most misunderstood requirements in the entire structure of CMM because the directions about how to move from Level 3 to Level 4 are very fuzzy.

The managed level is not merely about measurements; if it were, it would be called the measured level. Instead, Level 4 is about seeing and understanding the process as a whole by identifying interrelationships between subprocesses and managing them as they change. If Levels 2 and 3 are just a foundation for successful process management building, Level 4 provides a vision for the organization to control and finish construction of the building. Level 4 is an integration stage for all policies, procedures, and measurement practices implemented in the previous levels. Implementation of Level 4 KPAs allows management to predict not only the quality of the product, but the quality of its decisions.

Consider the story of three masons. A pedestrian asked three masons working on a construction project what they were doing. The first mason said, "I am laying bricks"; the second mason said, "I am building a wall"; and the third mason said, " I am building a temple to worship God."

Level 4 involves a dynamic set of subprocesses that is organized and internally directed toward certain goals. What are your goals? How productive have you been in achieving these goals? The process parameters should be defined first and measured second. The key elements of such a process include the following:

- Setting of subgoals that are instrumental to the achievement of higher level goals;

- Implementation of planned actions designed to coordinate the behavior of the process and its subprocesses to move them toward established goals;

- Management and monitoring of process performance so corrective actions can be taken if necessary.

Moving to Level 4 is very difficult and very time consuming, unless the organization starts implementation of measurement and metrics at the very beginning of the software process improvement.

Level 5: optimized

Continuous process improvement is enabled by quantitative feedback from the process and from testing innovative ideas and technologies [1]. In Level 5, the organization moves from the process improvement stage into the process management stage. Changes are monitored closely, using the measurement system, and the process is refined as needed. The organization operates at peak performance.

The keyword for Level 5 is *feedback*. It is not only a keyword, it is a concept. Management and its actions are part of the feedback process. Everybody shares responsibility for the problems associated with the process. No one person can be blamed.

You have to be very careful, though, with the feedback process. Why? It can limit your growth or push you back to the chaotic stage. The feedback should be goal oriented and balanced, otherwise you will fall into the trap of managing the changes that are wrong for your organization from the very beginning, and the process will feed itself with faulty information.

In the Level 5 organization, cycles are as regular as a daily commute.

> Commuter—one who spends his life
> In riding to and from his wife;
> A man who shaves and takes a train
> And then rides back to shave again.
>
> *E. B. White*

Benefits of the CMM approach

Do you remember the story of the Knights of the Round Table? The circle of the Round Table united its members with a set of common goals, ideas, and ethics—a common bond. After knights spent time at the Round Table, each of them went his own way, killing dragons and saving women, but their paths met, crossed, and intertwined [2].

CMM unites the software development organization and provides the following navigation and leadership tools with which management can improve the way in which they manage software projects:

- A clear understanding by software developers of what is expected of them. ("I have no idea what the customer really wants." "No one asked me if it is possible to implement this.")

- Clarity of work procedures and sufficiency of resources, skills, and knowledge. ("I do not have the training, the tools, the proper resources, or the time to do this job right.")

- Cross-functional processes that affect customer quality are defined. ("All I do is fix bugs.")

- Opportunities for improving the organization, process, and product quality. ("Hey, I tested *my* change, and it worked just fine in *my* environment.")

Common features of key process areas

The CMM's concept of common features is not really a new concept. In 1931, Walter Shewhart recognized that the outputs of manufacturing processes are subject to some types of variation, variations that cause excessive quality problems [4]. No two items going through a production line turned out exactly the same. The variations occurred as a result of imprecisions on the part of the machinery or the material or because of the skills of different machine operators. Shewhart called these *common causes* of variations and viewed them as a natural phenomenon in the production process. He developed methods for measuring variations and provided managers and workers the tools for determining whether their processes were operating smoothly or needed attention in order to improve quality.

On top of that, he recommended a course of action for each case. As a result, manufacturing personnel were able to identify the variations in a process and find ways to reduce them. This became known as the Shewhart cycle, and later reappeared in Japan under the name *kaisen* (continuous improvement). Don't you remember "Plan, Do, Check, and Act"?

Let's use the example of the Shewhart cycle as an analogy for our cause. CMM provides a structure for KPAs. This structure contains *common features;* is composed of goals, commitments, abilities, activities, measurements, and verification; and can serve as the main structure for software process improvement.

Goals

The goals stated in CMM are linked directly to the problems and opportunities of the software development organization.

For example, one CMM goal is the following: System requirements allocated to software are controlled to establish a baseline for software engineering and management use. Can you relate that goal to your business situation? Of course, you can. The requirements management problem is one of the most common problems in a software engineering community. In many companies the requirements are not controlled at all. They change all the way through the software development cycle, including the beta test.

Try to relate the KPA's goals to your business case. Very soon, you will realize that the problems you experience with your software development are the results of missing goals. Examples of typical problems include the following:

- Product delivery is late.

- The size and costs of the project keep increasing.

- The project is out of control.

- The product does not meet requirements.

- The performance of software subcontractors is poor.

This list, however, is endless.

Commitment to perform

This common feature usually involves establishment of organizational policies and requires senior management support. The key to this feature is to be able to establish a relationship between senior management and the actual people doing software process improvement using CMM as a guide.

Software process improvement is successful when the commitment of senior management is successfully tested. When senior management supports and encourages the members of a SEPG team, and gives them a good review from time to time, the effort of process improvement is going to succeed. If management's commitment is not truly strong, all improvement efforts are going to fall apart at the first sign of problems. The software improvement effort will die a slow death if management does not share commitment. As an example, I would like to quote one software development manager.

> We are not going to *mandate* the requirements management tool for this release. Instead, individual engineering managers can *choose* to use it if it helps them to meet their deliverables. If a manager believes the tool will aid in delivering on time with quality, he or she can use it and then demonstrate it to the rest of the organization for use on future products.

The degree of commitment of senior management is equal to the degree of risk the organization will take once it is committed to improving its processes and staying competitive in the marketplace. It is time for the top management to ask themselves a few questions.

- Does the organization have a vision, mission, goals, and objectives for the process improvement effort?

- How are they communicated?

- Are they written down?

Any attempt at software process improvement needs a stated goal. If there is no stated goal, the project will have no focus. In addition, a development organization with few policies and procedures will show inconsistent performance. This organization will go into the crisis mode at the first sign of a problem.

Policy statements generally refer to a written, organizational policy for the practices of that key process area. The policy should define responsibilities and authorities. The typical situation in most companies that are just beginning their software improvement efforts is that responsibilities are clear and authorities are not.

The policies and procedures handbook, if you choose to create one, should be a living document. This document is needed for short- and long-term planning. It will help to test the ideas, gain experience, and continuously improve the process.

Ability to perform

The ability to perform common feature describes the precondition that must exist in the project or organization to implement the software process competently. This simply means that you should have the abilities to do what you have planned and committed to do.

The level of detail of a documented procedure can vary significantly, from a handwritten individual desk procedure to a formal organizational standard operating procedure. The formality and level of detail depends on who will perform the task or activity (e.g., individual or team) and how often it is performed.

A documented procedure is usually needed so that the individuals responsible for a task or activity are able to perform it in a repeatable way and so that others with general knowledge of the area will be able to learn and perform the task or activity in the same way. This is an important aspect of institutionalizing a process.

Have you created the organizational structure to support project needs and software process improvement needs? One of the very important points that management needs to understand is that the organization should function and be managed as a system, not as a collection of independent subfunctions. Some organizations have unlimited funds for process improvement (I would love to see such a company). They can buy any tools for their "engineering sandbox." They can hire the best instructors in the world to teach their people new technology, but that organization will still be unable to improve anything without proper training of management in how to integrate individual performance goals into the overall organizational process of software development.

Activities performed

One hundred-and-fifty key practices fall under the activities performed common feature, representing almost half of the total number of key practices specified by CMM.

CMM is a descriptive not a prescriptive model. Activities performed vary from one organization to another. The implementation activities are different because the level of details, organizational focus, and need for planning and documentation are different. The focus of the CMM activities is on the software development process flow and requires procedures describing results to be accomplished.

Another important aspect of the CMM implementation is that you structure the activities around the tasks—not around the people. Your goal is to build a system that will allow continuous process improvement and be independent from any organizational changes involving people. Some companies that struggled through CMM implementation for some time found themselves in the situation of going down from Level 4 to Level 2 because the process improvement infrastructure was based on the effort and skills of individuals. The performed activities must be viewed and managed from a systems standpoint, not just management of an individual unit or function. What does it mean to manage activities from a system standpoint? It means that management should understand the relationship of their function in the software development life cycle to the total picture and define the entry and exit criteria for their part of the cycle.

Measurement and analysis

How do you know your development organization is doing things right? How are you measuring progress? How will you know how productive you are in achieving your goals or desired phase?

If your goals and objectives are specific and measurable, you can define measurements and metrics as a standard you can measure yourself.

Measurement and analysis is another common feature of KPA that describes the need to measure the process and analyze the measurements. The measurement and analysis section of CMM usually includes examples of the measurements that could be taken to determine the status and effectiveness of the activities performed.

The key practices in the measurement and analysis common feature describe basic measurement practices that are necessary to determine status related to the activities performed. The core suggested measures are in the areas of size, effort, schedule, and quality.

Verifying implementation

The verifying implementation common feature describes the steps to ensure that the activities are performed in compliance with the process that has been established. This common feature generally contains key practices that relate to oversight by senior management, project management, and software quality assurance.

The primary purpose of periodic reviews by senior management is to provide awareness of, and insight into, software process activities at an appropriate level of abstraction and in a timely manner. The time between reviews should meet the needs of the organization and may be lengthy, as long as adequate mechanisms for exception reporting are available.

The scope and content of senior management reviews depends in large part on which senior manager is involved in the review. Reviews by the senior manager responsible for all software project activities of an organization are expected to occur on a different schedule, and address different topics, in comparison with a review by the senior executive of the entire organization. Senior management reviews would also be expected to cover different topics, or similar topics at a higher level of abstraction, than project management oversight reviews.

Main process concepts of CMM

Software process definition

Software process definition is fundamental if higher levels of maturity are to be achieved. A fundamental concept of process definition in CMM is the organization's standard software process. An organization's standard software process is the operational definition of the basic process that guides the establishment of a common software process across the software projects in the organization. It describes the fundamental software process elements that each software project is expected to incorporate into its defined software process. It also describes the relationships (e.g., ordering and interfaces) between these software process elements. It establishes a consistent way of performing the software activities across the organization and is essential for long-term stability and improvement [1].

At the organizational level, the organization's standard software process needs to be described, managed, controlled, and improved in a formal manner. At the project level, emphasis is on the usability of the project's defined software process and the value it adds to the project. A project's defined software process is the operational definition of the software process used by the project. The project's defined software process is a well-characterized and understood software process, described in terms of software standards, procedures, tools, and methods. It is developed by tailoring the organization's standard software process to fit the specific characteristics of the project.

Process definition concepts

A fundamental concept that supports the approach taken by the SEI in its process definition work is that processes can be developed and maintained in a manner similar to the way in which products are developed and maintained. Requirements include a definition of the process to be described, an architecture and a design, implementation of the process design in a project or organizational situation, validation of the process description via measurement, and deployment of the process into widespread operation within the organization or project for which the process is intended.

Using the analogy of product development, a framework for software process development and maintenance has evolved that translates these concepts into ones that are more specific to the process development discipline (similar to the specificity of terminology used for developing real-time embedded systems versus management information systems) [1].

Organization's standard software process

An organization's standard software process is the operational definition of the basic process that guides the establishment of a common software process across the software projects in the organization. It describes the fundamental software process elements that each software project is expected to incorporate into its defined software process. It also describes the relationships (e.g., ordering and interfaces) between these software process elements. It guides the establishment of a common software process across the software development and maintenance projects in the organization.

The relationship between software process elements is sometimes referred to as a *software process architecture.*

The organization's standard software process forms the basis for a project's defined software processes. It provides continuity in the organization's process activities and is the reference for the measurements and long-term improvement of the software processes used in the organization [1].

Software process architecture

The software process architecture is a high-level (i.e., summary) description of the organization's standard software process. It describes the ordering, interfaces, interdependencies, and other relationships between the software process elements of the organization's standard software process. It also describes the interfaces, dependencies, and other relationships to other external processes (e.g., system engineering, hardware engineering, and contract management) [1].

Software process element

A software process element is a constituent element of a software process description. Each process element covers a well-defined, bounded, closely related set of tasks (e.g., software estimating element, software design element, coding element, and peer review element). The descriptions of the process elements may be templates to be filled in, fragments to be completed, abstractions to be refined, or complete descriptions to be modified or used unmodified.

A software life cycle is the period of time that begins when a software product is conceived and ends when the software is no longer available for use. The software life cycle typically includes a concept stage, requirements stage, design stage, implementation stage, test stage, installation and checkout stage, operation and maintenance stage, and, sometimes, a retirement stage.

Concepts related to the project's defined software process

Description

The description of a project's defined software process is the operational definition of the software process used by the project. The project's defined software process is a well-characterized and understood process, described in terms of software standards, procedures, tools, and methods. It has to be tailored to a standard software process that is accepted within the organization to fit specific characteristics of the project. This tailoring includes selecting a software life cycle model from the models already approved by the organization and modifying the organization's standard software process to fit the specific characteristics of the project.

The project's defined software process provides the basis for planning, performing, and improving activities of the managers and technical staff assigned to the project. It is possible for one project to have multiple defined software processes (e.g., for the operational software and for the test support software) or to have one defined software process for two or more similar projects.

Within the context of process definition, a task is a well-defined component of a defined process. All tasks can be considered activities, but not all activities are defined well enough to be considered tasks (although an activity may include a task). Because of this, use of the word *task* in the

Level 2 key practices is avoided and the less rigorous term *activity* is used. An activity is any step taken or function performed, both mental and physical, toward achieving some objective. Activities include all of the work the managers and technical staff do to perform the tasks of the project and organization.

The results of activities and tasks consist primarily of software work products. A software work product is any artifact created as part of defining, maintaining, or using a software process, including process descriptions, plans, procedures, computer programs, and associated documentation, which may or may not be intended for delivery to a customer or end user. Work products become inputs to the next step in the process or provide archival information on the software project for use in future projects.

Examples of software work products include plans, estimates, data on actual efforts, corrective action documentation, and requirements documents. The subset of software deliverables is referred to as software products [1].

Software products

The software products are the complete set, or any of the individual items of the set, of computer programs, procedures, and associated documentation and data designated for delivery to a customer or end user. All software products are also software work products. A software work product that will not be delivered to a customer or end user is not, however, a software product.

The description of the project's defined software process will usually not be specific enough to be performed directly. Although the description typically identifies such things as roles (i.e., who performs a task) and types of software work products needed to perform a task, it does not specify the individual who will assume the roles, the specific software work products that will be created, nor the schedule for performing the tasks and activities.

The project's software development plan, either as a single document or a collection of plans collectively referred to as a software development plan, provides the bridge between the project's defined software process (what will be done and how it will be done) and the specifics of how the project will be performed (e.g., which individuals will produce which software work products according to what schedule). The combination of the project's defined software process and its software development plan makes it possible to actually perform the process [1].

Key practices and the CMM

The key practices are not meant to limit the choice of a software life cycle. People who have extensively used one particular software life cycle may perceive elements of that life cycle in the organization and structure of the key practices. However, there is no intent either to encourage or preclude the use of any particular software life cycle.

The term *stage* is used to refer to a defined partition of the software project's effort, but the term should not be tied to any specific software life cycle. As it is used in the key practices, *stage* can mean rigidly sequential stages or overlapping and iterative stages.

The key practices neither require nor preclude specific software technologies, such as prototyping, object-oriented design, or reuse of software requirements, design, code, or other elements.

The key practices describe a number of process-related documents, each one covering specific areas of content. The key practices do not require a one-to-one relationship between the documents named in the key practices and the actual work products of an organization or project; nor is there an intended one-to-one relationship to documents specified by the U.S. Department of Defense or to standards such as DOD-STD-2167A or IEEE software standards. The key practices require only that the applicable contents of these documents be part of the organization's or project's written work products.

Collection and analysis of process data

The key practices for the collection and analysis of the process data evolve across the maturity levels.

At Level 2, the data are primarily related to the size of the project's work products, effort, and schedule, and are defined, collected, and stored separately by each project. The data are shared between projects via informal procedures [1].

At Level 3, each project has a defined software process tailored from the organization's standard software process. Data related to each project's defined software process are collected and stored in the organization's software process database. The data collected and stored may be different for each project, but the data are well defined within the organization's software process database [1].

At Level 4, the organization defines a standard set of measurements based on the organization's standard software process. All projects collect this standard set of measurement data, as well as other project-specific data, and store them in the organization's software process database. The data are used by the projects to quantitatively understand and stabilize the process performance of the project's defined software processes. They are also used by the organization to establish a process capability baseline for the organization's standard software process [1].

At Level 5, data are used to select areas for technology and process improvements, to plan these improvements, and to evaluate the effects of these improvements on the organization's process capability [1].

Applying professional judgment

To provide a complete set of valid principles that apply to a wide range of situations, some of the key practices are intentionally stated to allow for flexibility. Throughout the key practices, nonspecific phrases like "affected groups," "as appropriate," and "as necessary" are used. The use of such nonspecific terms is generally minimized in the key practices, with examples provided in many cases, at least for the first use of the term. These phrases may have different meanings for two different organizations, for two projects in a single organization, or for one project at different points in its life cycle. Each project or organization must clarify these phrases for its specific situation.

Clarifying these phrases requires the organization to consider the overall context in which they are used. The pertinent question is whether the specific interpretation of one of these phrases meets the goals of the

KPA. Professional judgment must be used to determine whether the goals have been achieved.

Professional judgment must also be used when interpreting the key practices and how they contribute to the goals of a key process area. In general, the KPAs describe a fundamental set of behaviors that all software organizations should exhibit, regardless of their size or their products.

The key practices in the CMM, however, must be interpreted in light of a project or organization's business environment and specific circumstances. This interpretation should be based on an informed knowledge of both the CMM and the organization and its projects. The goals of the KPAs provide a means for structuring this interpretation. If an organization's implementation of a key process area satisfies the goals, but differs significantly from the key practices, the rationale for the interpretation should be documented. A documented rationale will help assessment and evaluation teams understand why certain practices are implemented the way they are.

Applying professional judgment leads to the issue of the "goodness" of the software process. The CMM does not place "goodness" requirements on the software process, although it does establish minimal criteria for a "reasonable" process in many software environments. The objective of process management is to establish processes that are used and can act as a foundation for systematic improvement based on the organization's business needs.

References

[1] Paulk, M. C., et al., *The Capability Maturity Model: Guidelines for Improving the Software Process,* Reading, MA: Addison-Wesley, 1995.

[2] Senge, P., *The Fifth Discipline,* New York: Currency Doubleday, 1990, p. 21.

[3] Hansen, G. A., *Automating Business Process Reengineering,* Englewood Cliffs, NJ: Prentice Hall, 1997.

[4] Shewhart, W., *Economic Control of Quality of Manufactured Product,* 1931.

Assessments and What the Assessors Are Seeking

All things are full of labor; man cannot utter it: the eye is not satisfied
with seeing, nor the ear filled with hearing.

Ecclesiastes 1:8

Software development processes

There are two methods suggested by SEI for the software process
appraisal: software process assessment and software capability evaluation
(SCE). The objective is to evaluate the organization in the same manner,
using CMM's criteria.

No matter what method of appraisal you are using, the main idea is to evaluate the processes associated with management decision making, communications, and technical support. Assessment is a very important tool with which to establish a baseline for your organization's way of developing software.

Assessors do not evaluate the technical soundness of the product you built; instead, they are concerned with how you plan, estimate, and communicate. What do you document and measure? When is the next software quality assurance (SQA) audit and peer review meeting scheduled? Do you know who is in charge? The quality of software implementation depends on the quality of management and the quality of decision making.

What criteria are used for the evaluation and determination of the efficiency of the process? Is your process efficient and functional? Evaluators cannot evaluate how much blood, sweat, and tears you devote to project implementation. Evaluators are looking for the evidence of a software process that is effective in building the organizational capability and that satisfies most of the requirements of CMM. It should be practiced, documented, enforced, trained, measured, and able to be improved.

Did your organization establish a software process for software estimating? Does it constitute a reasonable process? Is it documented and consistently followed and controlled? There is a large volume of information that should be collected and reviewed by evaluators in order to make accurate decisions regarding the efficiency of your operations. The software life cycle is a process of performing necessary activities. It includes not only software development activities but also multiple related activities such as operations, planning, and estimation. Assessors evaluate the process by these means:

- Visit the organization for four or five days. The length of the visit depends on what levels will be evaluated.

- Complete two to four project examinations at the company site.

- Interview development staff and management.

- Read supporting documentation.

- Produce findings by means of a consensus delineating strengths and weaknesses.

The attention of evaluators is directed toward very specific activities performed on both periodic and event-driven bases. The phrase "on both periodic and event-driven bases" is used in key practices to emphasize that projects need different types of reviews at different stages, depending on the project characteristics. "Project management should maintain an ongoing awareness of the status of the software effort and be informed when significant events on the software project occur. Examples include project management participation in formal reviews, such as critical design reviews, as well as reviews which encompass process issues such as status of process improvement planning and resolution of process non-compliance issues" [1].

At the project level, project management review is expected to be more detailed than that of senior management, reflecting project management's more active involvement in the operational aspects of a project.

How the organization models, measures, and controls the unstable behavior of a software life cycle is a long-recognized problem, one that attracts a lot of attention from evaluators. Assessing the organization is like assessing personalities: Ask a question and wait for the response. Each question demands a factual answer, and these can only be obtained through analysis and investigation. If objective answers are obtained, then the evaluator's decision is much less likely to be faulty.

Evaluators' questions can best be answered by presenting software metrics and management reports based on the tracking of quantitative data. Using a quantitative approach can help you not only to identify needed metrics, but at the same time to provide assistance in preparation for the evaluation. Examples of typical evaluators' questions and possible ways your organization can respond follow.

Is a formal procedure used to ensure periodic management review of the status of each software development process? The organizational responsibilities of project managers are defined and project managers regularly review the status of the project. Show the existence of a size, cost, and schedule estimating procedure and demonstrate that the procedure has been used. Action items from management review are tracked and analyzed, data collected, and metrics presented.

Present to evaluators metrics and reports prepared for the management review of software development. Rework metrics could be very useful. The information from rework metrics can be viewed on a daily, weekly, or monthly basis, making software development reviews simple.

For each project, are independent audits conducted for each step of the software development process? Your organization should have a separate SQA reporting chain. You should be able to prove the existence of trained and sufficient resources to audit all phases of the software development life cycle.

Software quality assurance activities

The particular activities that are considered appropriate for review and/or audit by the SQA group are described as a key practice. For some particular cases, SQA verification activities are not described, such as for the training program and intergroup coordination KPAs. These types of KPAs are at the boundary between the software project and the organization, where the SQA group would not be expected to have authority.

The idea of an independent audit is to measure project compliance with the project's criteria, which laid out the schedule, a budget, and the quality target. If you have measurement tools, you can track the software development cycle from the beginning and monitor it periodically. Reports and metrics should be generated to provide all of the information needed for an independent audit.

Are the coding standards applied to each software development project? Coding standards can easily be tracked through many different metrics. The fault removal process and the quality level can be monitored via rework metrics. Code growth and code changes can be tracked via volatility metrics. Complexity metrics reports can be generated on specific metric counts; for instance, a report can be generated for all functions with cyclomatic complexity greater than 10, and the flow of the project or piece of a project can be seen and monitored.

Is a formal procedure used to produce software development schedules? Software development schedules can be estimated more efficiently by taking a historical look at the organization's previous efforts on similar projects.

Are formal procedures applied to estimating software development costs? Calibrated software estimation tools, such as SLIM and SLIM CONTROL (Quantitative Software Management, Inc., or QSM), that are supported by historical data about the costs and effort of the previous project will help you answer the question. But, do not forget that software estimation is a continual process and should be continually tracked and updated. The data from each step should be used to improve the estimation process.

Are software staffing profiles maintained that reflect actual staffing versus planned staffing? The staffing profiles metrics can be very helpful when trying to convince evaluators that you make resource allocation decisions based on factual information.

Are profiles of software size maintained for each software configuration item, over time? Information about the software size should be available at any level of the project for any period within a project, whether you are working with a single module, subsystem, or the entire project. All of the sizing information should be kept in the project repository and updated as needed for as long as the project is kept in the system. The benefits of such an approach are clear.

- Control of the developmental baseline;

- Change and configuration control mechanism;

- Traceability between different product phases.

Are statistics on software coding and test errors gathered? A number of software reliability metrics are available to track coding and testing errors generated through the project, and to generate information such as mean time to failure (MTTF) and mean time to repair (MTTR). Early in the development process, fault profiles can be used to measure the quality of the translation of the software requirements to the design stage. Later in the development process, they can be used to measure the quality of the implementation of the software design to the code stage.

Are profiles maintained of actual versus planned software units designed, over time? The design profiles can be monitored through design stability metrics. Design stability is used to indicate the amount of change being made to the design of the software. The design progress ratio typically shows how the completeness of the design is progressing over time and helps give an indication of how to view the stability in relation to the total projected design.

Are profiles maintained of actual versus planned software units that were completed and tested over time? Depth and breadth of testing metrics are very useful for addressing the degree to which required functionality has been successfully demonstrated and the amount of testing achieved on software architecture. Those two metrics help users keep track of the completed and tested software units. They complement a configuration management system, which provides data on the tested units of code.

Is target computer input/output (I/O) channel utilization tracked? The computer resource utilization metric shows the degree to which estimates and measurements of the target computer resources (CPU capacity, memory and storage capacity, and I/O capacity) are used, changing or approaching the limits of resource availability. Overutilization of computer resources can have a serious impact on costs, scheduling, and supportability. Proper use of metrics can also ensure that each resource in a system has adequate reserve to allow for future growth due to changing or additional requirements without requiring redesign.

Are software trouble reports being generated from the testing through closure stages? A software problem report system usually tracks trouble reports via date detected, date assigned, and date closed. The fault profile metric is a summary software problem or change report that has been collected by the system. You track continuously the number and type of faults to closure, as well as developers' abilities to fix problems.

Does senior management have a mechanism for the regular review of the status of software development projects? Teach your management the methodology of metrics usage, interpretation, and correlation of information, which will provide a solid ground for decision making.

Is a mechanism used for controlling changes to the software requirements? A mechanism should be in place to control changes to software requirements. Requirements modifications should be assessed and understood before a commitment to implement them is made. Change control helps to ensure that all requirements documents and the requirements traceability matrix are maintained properly. These documents can then be used to ensure accurate project planning, complete documentation, and useful test planning.

Is a software engineering process group function in place? By implementing measurement procedures and metrics tools, the analysis and reporting capabilities will aid a software engineering process group if one is not already in place.

Is the required software engineering training program for software developers in place? The use of metric tools could act as a training aid for software developers to learn the software engineering process as well as organizational standards quickly and easily.

Is a formal training program required for design and code review leaders? With the use of easy-to-understand graphics and reports of the measurement/metrics tool, the training required for design and code review will be greatly reduced.

Does the software organization use a standardized and documented software development process on each project? By implementing measurement/metrics tools, all software development projects can be tracked. This gives the organization a head start on standardizing their software development process.

Does the standard development process documentation describe the use of tools and techniques? Good measurement/metrics tools should have a complete documentation set that can be used to train the entire organization on the function of the tool, techniques, theory, and analysis methods.

Is a mechanism used for assessing existing designs and code for reuse in new applications? One of the most important issues involved in applications reuse is the issue of what functions or modules will the easiest to maintain and modify. Metrics tool can help in many different ways. One of them is reviewing different cyclomatic (functional) complexity metrics, as well as structural flow.

Are code maintainability standards applied? Complexity metrics can generate reports showing complexity levels for all modules. This information can then be analyzed to determine what is maintainable.

Are statistics on software design errors gathered? These statistics can be gathered through rework and design stability metrics.

Is a mechanism used for identifying and resolving system engineering issues that affect software? By using different metrics such as complexity, reliability, and volatility, system engineering issues can be cross-referenced and analyzed for each module of software.

Is a mechanism used for independently calling integration and test issues to the attention of the project manager? Integration and testing issues can be tracked on a periodic basis to make the project manager aware of any potential problems that may affect the cost, quality, or schedule of the project. The tracking could be accomplished through the correlation of the different types of information coming from the metrics such as complexity, reliability, and rework.

Is a mechanism used to ensure compliance with the software engineering standards? Metrics tools cannot ensure that an organization is in compliance with the standards, but management and team leaders can track the issues through the different reports and graphs generated by a metrics tool.

Is a mechanism used for ensuring traceability between software requirements, top-level design, software detailed design, and the code? The use of a requirements traceability matrix will help to establish a disciplined process under project management control. The goal of the requirements management process is to ensure that the product requirements are complete, verifiable, consistent, traceable, and testable. The requirements traceability matrix identifies the documents selected for tracing and should contain enough information to allow assessment of the traceability between various levels of requirements and the requirements for their design and test cases.

Are formal records maintained of unit (module) development progress? The connection between the source code control system and the metrics tool will help to maintain information on module development progress. A metrics tool should be able to keep the records of all module development progress, so that you can display the information for any one module at any time in the process.

Are software code reviews conducted? Software code reviews can be conducted on a periodic basis through such metrics as volatility, reliability, and complexity to track any issues of size, quality, faults, or structure.

Is a mechanism used for verifying that the samples examined for software quality assurance are truly representative of the work performed? The metrics technologies allow information to be viewed for a specific sampling period. Through graphics, the testing cycle can be easily determined, giving a true sampling period for the SQA group's verification needs.

Is there a mechanism for ensuring the adequacy of regression testing? Regression testing can be analyzed through the reliability and testing metrics. By setting predetermined quality goals and objectives, the progress of regression testing can be tracked easily.

Is a mechanism used for deciding when to insert new technology into the development process? Metrics tools do not decide when to insert new technology. By performing a historical analysis and taking a look at the process, it is possible to find supporting information to aid in that type of decision making.

Is a mechanism used for managing and supporting the introduction of new technologies? While the metrics tools do not manage and support and introduction of the new technologies, they can provide the means to measure the effect on quality, productivity, and cost from the introduction of the new technologies.

Are code review standards applied? Code review standards can be tracked by the metrics tool by generating different reports in order to make sure that the standards are being followed.

Are design errors projected and compared to actual? The design stability metrics and rework metrics can solve that issue.

Are coding and test errors projected and compared to actual? Errors can be projected through reliability technology for all parts of the process. The fault tracking system generates reports on actual errors that can, in turn, be compared to projected results over time.

Are design and code review coverage measured and recorded? The metrics tool should provide the mechanism to measure code coverage through different metrics such as design progress and development progress.

Is test coverage measured and recorded for each phase of functional testing? Testing coverage should be measured and recorded for all phases of functional testing. The breadth of a testing metric can be used to represent three different measures of functional test progress.

1. Test coverage (the percentage of the approved software requirements baseline that has been tested);

2. Test success (the percentage of functional tests that passed);

3. Overall success (the percentage of the approved software requirements baseline that passed testing).

Has a managed and controlled process database been established for process metrics data across all projects? The primary purpose of any metrics tool is to be able to control the process metric data across all projects. It should provide automated data collection and be able to store the data in a data repository, making any or all of this information available at any time in the project life cycle.

Are the error data from code reviews and tests analyzed to determine the likely distribution and characteristics of the errors remaining in a product? Through the reliability metrics, the calculation of total predicted faults is possible. Using this information from the software problem report system, distribution of errors remaining in the project can easily be determined.

Are analyses of errors conducted to determine their process-related causes? Errors can be analyzed to determine process-related causes through analyzing sizing information and test coverage with volatility and reliability metrics, as well as complexity counts and structural flow.

Is a mechanism used for identifying and replacing obsolete technologies? A historical analysis can be performed on previous projects that will help determine obsolete technologies by measuring their effect on quality and productivity.

Is a mechanism used for error collection analysis? Errors can be attributed to many different factors. One way to perform error cause analysis is to analyze the correspondence of the complexity parameters and the number of faults in a particular module. This information can be gathered through the metrics.

Are error causes reviewed to determine what process changes are required to prevent them? Once error causes are determined, a historical look at the process will aid in determining where the process must change to prevent further errors.

Is a mechanism used for initiating error prevention actions? Through the error cause analysis, a correlation between the complexity and reliability information can be established. Metrics reports can be generated and reviewed in order to prevent further errors.

Assessment

It is very difficult to make a decision about the strengths and weaknesses of your organization because of the large amounts of information presented. This is why the major investigative vehicle of any assessment is the interview.

Question: "Would you please describe how you plan for software development on your project?"

Answer: "You go. You talk. You do."

What the interviewer expects: "From allocated requirements we derive estimates of size, costs, and schedules. We document the software development plan, which is approved by the senior management and controlled by project managers."

Question: "How do you derive project estimates?"

Answer: "All software developers who will be involved in the project analyze the requirements and provide an estimate based on their understanding of how long it should take."

What the interviewer expects: "Our estimates are based on historical information kept in the database. Size, effort, costs, schedules, and lessons learned from past projects are documented and serve as a basis for the new estimates."

Question: "How do you track progress against your project's software plan?"

Answer: "If the software is late for integration, we call an emergency meeting to resolve the critical issues and change the content of the build proposal."

What the interviewer expects: "We collect the measurements on size, effort, costs, schedules, and actual critical resource utilization. We analyze the deviations from the plan. We monitor the potential risk. The goals summarize the key practices, which, in turn, describe a reasonable software process."

Question: "Please describe when and how you take corrective actions to reduce the deviations from the plan."

Answer: ????? (puzzled silence).

What the interviewer expects: "We revise, update, and reestimate the development plan when corrective actions are taken. We review the situation before corrective actions are taken. We identify, document, and monitor technical, cost, and resource risks."

Table 3.1 shows an example of typical questions for a program or project manager. Note how one question correlates to more than one KPA.

Table 3.1

Typical Program or Project Manager Questions and the
Related KPA

Question	KPA
Please describe your role in this project and the following information about this project: Status? Customer? Relationship with customer?	SPP SPTO
How do you exercise control over your project (cost, schedule, quality)? Who controls the project? What types of status reports do you make to management? Are there standards for software development? How do you know that standards are followed? How do you know that requirements are met?	RM SPP SPTO SPE
Please tell us about your staff: Experience? Personnel turn over?	SPP SPTO TP
Can you describe the planning process (size, cost, schedule estimation)? Resources available? Staff qualification?	SPP TP
How do you select subcontractors? How do you measure their progress?	SSM
How do you ensure the quality product is delivered to your customers?	SQA
Can you describe the SPI activities in your organization?	OPD, OPF
How do you assess and mitigate your program risk?	ISM
Please describe the role of SCM in your program.	SCM
What is your interaction with SQA?	SQA

Misconceptions of CMM

CMM will not drastically improve organizational productivity, quality, and bottom line overnight. You can work on improvements for all levels in parallel. CMM does not address every issue that makes a software project successful. CMM is concerned with organizational process capability. It does not pass judgment on the performance or capabilities of the practitioners.

You do not have to compile piles and piles of documentation for the assessors; just make sure that the information presented has enough data to convince assessors that projects are planned and managed. Information should identify activities that will be or already are performed on a project in order to minimize the risk associated with the project performance. Do not generate wasteful paperwork just for the showcase. Assessors are looking for specific information, such as files containing peer review notes, or project metrics associated with the software project management or project tracking and oversight.

Postevaluation

In many cases, the assessment of the projects and their organization from the CMM perspective serves as a very good way to educate senior management. SCE findings do not only represent project status, as identified by the strengths and weaknesses of the organization; sometimes the organization is a long way from where it wants to be or thinks it is. The objectivity of the evaluation is important, as well as educating the audience, so the consensus is achieved not only inside of the evaluators' team, but with the audience.

It is very important to understand that a good evaluation report focus on facts presented by the organization (by *you*).

In some cases the assessment involves delivering news that is not pleasant for the audience to hear. No one likes to be told how all of the effort and resources poured into implementation of the CMM levels did not exactly pay off. In many cases, companies ignore the messengers—because they cannot shoot them!

The object of evaluation is not to lay blame for the errors of the past nor to criticize past decisions; the object is not to point fingers at any one manager whose project does not comply with the CMM requirements. The objective of the assessment of a company's software development capabilities is to lay a foundation for future planning, which must be done to satisfy the five levels of CMM.

CMM objectives and organizational focus

That which is crooked cannot be made straight; and that which is wanting cannot be numbered.

Ecclesiastes 1:15

We do not measure quality of process improvement anymore, we measure quickness.

Doug Hill

How significant is CMM implementation for your organization? Does it match the objectives of your organization in general and individual projects or departments specifically? Is your concern software process improvement or CMM levels? Are you a commercial company developing shrink-wrapped software, or are you are working on the proposal for a new government contract?

In any case, common sense and timing should work for you. You have to be aware of, understand, and evaluate the goals of the individual functions and the organization as a whole (see Table 3.2).

The goals in Table 3.2 seem to be so overwhelming that any effort related to software process improvement is a scary thought. One engineering manager stated in his memo: "We do not have time to mandate, train, and implement significant process changes at this point for this project just to get to Level 2. We just went through a horrendously painful exercise of cutting a bunch of this release out in order to alleviate risk due to attrition fears. I am not willing to put more back on the table (you can quote me on that)."

The focus of any organization and of underlying objectives is not how to achieve a high CMM level; the objective is to initiate software process improvement in order to stay competitive in business. You have to recognize what is worth changing and improving. How would you really like to manage a software development organization?

Table 3.2
Organizational Functions and Goals

Function	Goals
Program management	Set costs
	Set schedules
	Monitor customer satisfaction
Project management	Keep the project within budgeted cost and schedule
	Deliver high-quality product
	Provide communication and coordination between customers, developers, and different departments
Software management	Keep project within budget and schedule
	Identify potential risks and volatility
	Monitor product quality
	Deliver required functionality
Software development	Complete project assignments on time
	Develop high quality product
	Communication and coordination
	Improve the development process
System integration	Verify requirement traceability and testability
	Integrate third-party product and verify quality (reliability)
	Communicate and coordinate
Software quality	Audit development processes
	Document the corrective actions

The problem of any organization is that we are all in a rush to improve processes and become a mature organization as soon as possible. Everybody is dealing with a lot of things that had to be done yesterday. Sometimes we have to stop and take a close look what is going on in the organization. We have to start focusing. Focusing is turning the attention to a specific situation and seeing it as if for the first time.

Do not be fooled if your division or company is at Level 3 or Level 4. Do not get hooked on labels. One organization went from Level 4 to Level 1 in 12 months.

Use the CMM structure to support your fight for competitiveness. Use the CMM structure as a process model for defining, changing, and improving. If, at the present time, you are enjoying success in the software development business, it is not going to last forever if your development is not structured and you cannot quantify your successful performance. This is not your success; this is the success of your marketing organization. Most software development organizations assume that tomorrow will be exactly like yesterday. They believe that the changes will be unpredictable and will be introduced very slowly. They believe that the process of software development is a highly individual process, an art that cannot be planned or managed. They do not focus their efforts on making software development organizations cost effective. Try to calculate, as a fun exercise, how much you pay for your software maintenance effort. How much do you have to pay to fix one software bug reported from the customer site? Now multiply that number by the number of bugs located in a bug-reporting database.

Figure 3.1 demonstrates how the software process improvement and the CMM concept fit into the organizational competitiveness model. Organizational competitiveness is a result of many contributing factors. One of them is organizational commitment to improve the cost effectiveness of the individual departments through process improvement. An organization makes a commitment to improve the process, document it in specific policies, and create the necessary environment for policy enforcement and verification of the process activities. The nature of process improvement is the verification of the activities related to the product development or process improvement throughout the organizational environment.

The next level is process-measurement concurrence. Integration of the process-measurement framework provides the organization with a mechanism not only to implement the software process improvement concept, but to be able to solve other potential issues using measurements and metrics, which can relate to other parts of the business.

The bottom level is a procedure-interpretation framework. Developing the abilities of one part of the organization can be different from doing so for other parts. The same developed procedures must be subject to interpretation and should be modified accordingly. What works for one group of people will not work for the other. The group culture can be different, the skills can be different, and the product requirements can

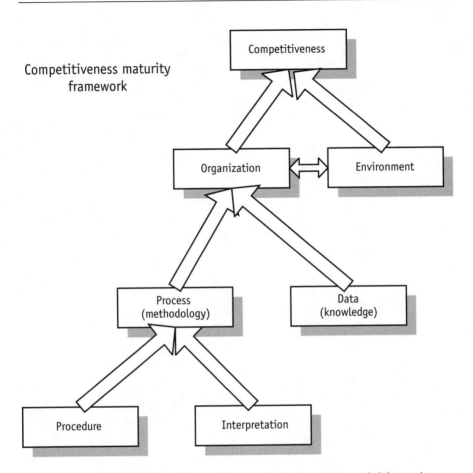

Figure 3.1 Fitting the software process improvement model into the competitiveness model.

be different. Procedures should not be used as a dogma, but should display needed flexibility, which will allow necessary interpretation.

Reference

[1] Paulk, M. C., et al., *The Capability Maturity Model: Guidelines for Improving the Software Process,* Reading, MA: Addison-Wesley, 1995.

Process Focus

Those who really seek the path of Enlightenment dictate terms to their mind. Then they proceed with strong determination.

Buddha

A process focus

Any software development organization is a system, a social system. If you are a part of the system, either as a software engineer or a project manager, it is necessary to understand how the system is operating. It is difficult to generalize software development organizations because companies are different, projects are different, and people are different. One thing, however, is very common: the combination of technology and people. It is difficult enough to manage technology with the new and continuous advances, but when people are added to the equation you end up with a very complex structure. People, working on a software project, react differently and unpredictably to the same set of problems that need solving. All people in software development organizations have a common goal: to deliver a high-quality product on schedule and within budget to the customer. At the same time, the software development organization is very volatile organization, sometimes with a big turnover rate and many problems. "If you dig very deeply into any problem, you will get to 'people'" [1]. Let us now go to the roots.

In his book *The Synergism Hypothesis,* Peter Corning gives two examples from Adam Smith's *Wealth of Nations* [2]. In the first example, Adam Smith described a pin factory that he personally observed in which 10 workers together were able to produce 48,000 pins per day. They did this by dividing the production process into component tasks, each of which lent itself to specialization. If each worker were to work alone, attempting to perform all of the tasks associated with making pins, Smith thought it unlikely that on any given day they would be able to produce even one pin per worker.

We can look at the pin factory in another way by considering how various specialized skill and production operations were combined in an organized, goal-oriented system. The system described included not only the roles played by the 10 workers. Those roles had to be precisely articulated with respect to one another. The description included the appropriate machinery, the energy to run the machinery, sources of raw materials, a supporting transportation system, and markets in which production costs are recovered through sales. Finally, the pin factory operation was also dependent on an existing communication and control subsystem (on top of the technical advances) through which planning, the hiring and training of workers, production decisions and coordination, marketing, and bookkeeping could be effected. The success of the pin factory was the result of the total organization, the total configuration of functional relationships between worker and worker, worker and machine, worker and society, and worker and environment. Remove any one of these components and the system, as a system of cooperative interaction and interdependencies management, would not work.

In the second example, Smith compared the transport of goods overland from London to Edinburgh in "broad-wheeled" wagons and the transport of goods by sailing ships between London and Leith, the seaport that serves Edinburgh. In six weeks, two men and eight horses could deliver about four tons of goods to Edinburgh and back. In the same amount of time, a ship with a crew of six or eight men could carry 200 tons to Leith—an amount of freight that would require 50 wagons, 100 men, and 400 horses for overland transport.

What was the critical difference here? It was not the division of labor alone; not the technical advances embodied in ships as opposed to horses and wagons; not the capital needed to finance the building of ship. It was, in part, all of these things: the total configuration of factors integrated in one system and one process associated with shipborne commerce. They created a system that tied together a number of formerly independent operations. They created a system of people for allocating resources and regulating activities of the business. Later that system was called *business process management*. They understood the process interdependence to mean that all of the different skills involved led to recognition of a common goal [2].

One more example illustrates achievement of the main goal by setting incremental subgoals. Setting subgoals enhances the adaptability of the process. This example was described by Herbert Simon [3]. Once there were two watchmakers, Hora and Tempus, who manufactured very fine watches. Both of them were highly regarded, and the phones in their workshops rang frequently because new customers were constantly calling. However, Hora prospered, while Tempus became poorer and poorer and finally lost his shop. What was the reason? The watches the men made consisted of about 1,000 parts each. Tempus constructed his watches so that if he had one partially assembled and had to put it down—say, to answer the phone—it immediately fell to pieces and had to be reassembled from the separate elements. The better the customers liked his watches, the more they phoned him, and the more difficult it became for him to find enough uninterrupted time to finish a watch.

The watches that Hora made were no less complex than those of Tempus, but Hora had designed them so that he could put together subassemblies of about 10 elements each. Ten of these complete subassemblies, then, could be put together into a larger subassembly; a system of 10 of the later subassemblies constituted the whole watch. Hence, when Hora had to put down a partially assembled watch in order to answer the phone, he lost only a small part of his work, and he assembled his watches in only a fraction of the man-hours it took Tempus.

In this example Hora organized the components into a stable subsystem and therefore created a process that was flexible enough to adapt to outside disturbances. What is most important to understand is that Hora set up systematic subgoals, which were then translated into the interdependent subassemblies. Setting subgoals led to achievement of the ultimate final goal, which was not attainable otherwise. Hora was able to achieve success in three very important steps of gaining knowledge.

- *Step One:* Obtain knowledge of how each individual part works.

- *Step Two:* Obtain knowledge of how each part works with those to which it is connected.

- *Step Three:* Obtain knowledge of how all of these interactions combine in the system to produce the desired effect.

If we assume for a second that Hora is a software development manager, he probably will go through the same three steps to understand how a particular software development process works in order to ensure the quality of developed software at the budgeted cost.

- *Step One:* Collect primitive data to analyze potential problems.

- *Step Two:* Present the collected data using software metrics.

- *Step Three:* Integrate software metrics into the indicators for visibility into important issues.

These indicators will cover all phases of the software development life cycle and provide meaningful information for the software developers as well as management.

Going back to our example, Hora comes to the conclusion that there is no point in measuring the individual's performance because the developers' contribution is integrated with the work of others. In the software development organization, one individual has very little control over the quality of the product (we are not talking about extreme cases, such as unqualified people), but the development team and communication between members of the team have everything to do with the quality of the product.

Process management for results

Traditionally, managers of software projects are preoccupied with management by results. It is normal for the software development organization, where sometimes inconsistent and unpredictable tasks require specific skills, to be managed by the release date. This situation creates an environment that is difficult to manage and to work in. This environment is highly reactive and keeps the team of developers in a firefighting mode all the time. I hope you remember the old joke that applies to this type of environment. A guy meets a friend and says: "I am sorry, I heard you had a fire in your store." The friend's response: "Sshh . . . it is tomorrow." In this environment, the software project data are not managed or understood and therefore are not used as the basis for management reviews. When the release date is around the corner and the number of features still to be developed is overwhelming, the original project plan goes down the drain. From this moment on, the project is not controlled and its success depends heavily on a few individuals working day and night trying to save the release. The problem is that the overall release environment is viewed as a set of individual tasks as well as specific product and process knowledge, resulting in many unresolved issues. Developers' practices and tasks are not well defined and measured in terms of effectiveness and efficiency.

The situation we have just described is not a system of managed processes based on a common goal. It is a clear way to failure, particularly if the organization is facing the situation of reduced development cycle time to bring a quality product to market with limited resources.

Can we eliminate all problems in software development? Probably not; problems are normal for any given stage of the development life cycle. Nevertheless, they are predictable and can be controlled by management. Management can deal with them and control the flow of the software development process. What kills the development process is a different set of problems. These problems are created when management does not face a problem to begin with and later is not capable of dealing with the ripple effect of failing quality, cost, and schedule performance.

Management has to find a way to continuously prevent, understand, and solve the problems before they have a devastating effect. Analyzing the problems will help us to understand that problems are not caused by individuals but by the situation. It is not the fault of an individual if the required software requirements are not identified or if applicable standards are not applied or effectively tailored. It is not the fault of an individual if the quality of the product falls behind. These types of problems are the result of the poor quality process. Why improve and manage processes? For these reasons:

- Processes produce organizational products.

- Processes are critical to maintaining a competitive edge.

- Processes are the vehicles for meeting customer needs.

- Processes are critical in achieving organizational goals.

"The performance of individuals is only as good as the processes allow it to be." Therefore, if the management of the software development organization wants to minimize the number of problems it is constantly facing, it has to change its focus and learn how to "manage for results and by the process." The effect of change will give the organization a sense of control.

The Mulla sent a small boy to get water from the well. "Make sure you don't break the pot!" he shouted and gave the child a clout. "Mulla," asked the spectator, "why do you strike someone who hasn't done anything wrong?" "Because, you fool," said the Mulla, "it would be too late to punish him after he broke the pot, wouldn't it?"

If the process manages the organization, the organization can achieve continuous improvement, which, in addition, will be measurable. The process-focused approach means that attention is concentrated on the process, rather than the product. For example, you would be able to identify (using schedule metrics planned versus actual schedule) that your project is behind schedule and that the number of defects discovered is not acceptable. You then adjust the process, making sure that the design specifications contain enough detail, which helps developers translate designs into accurate code more easily. If instead you decide to increase the test cycle to improve the quality after the fact, you are using a product-focused approach.

What represents advancement in a process-focused approach?

- Progressive increases in data collection;

- Development of measurement capabilities;

- Analysis of informational content;

- Subprocess interdependency management.

These parameters interact with and influence each other in many ways.

Let us look at the definition of the software development process stated by SEI: "A software process is a set of activities, methods, practices, and transformations that people use to develop and maintain software products" [4].

To improve product quality, the process of software development should be understood, defined, measured, and continuously improved. New software process technologies are being developed to address the areas of process assessment, definition, simulation, and implementation. Here are a few interpretations of some common statements:

- Software process *assessment* is the act of determining the maturity of an organization's software process.

- Software process *definition* is the act of specifying a process in detail. Software process *simulation* is the act of executing a software process definition.

- The term *modeling* is often used to encompass both process definition and simulation. The process implementation emphasizes the use of a formal process definition to guide and control the software process.

To manage the software engineering organization by means of a process-focused approach, management should have the capabilities to identify, understand, and solve potential problems. Good management should make good decisions and efficiently implement them because management is only as good as the decisions it makes.

Components of the management decision process

> The cause is well hidden, but the result is well known.
>
> *Anonymous*

Three components of information go into the decision process. For any project manager, these components are goals, constraints, and alternatives. Goals are what every project manager wants out of the process of software development: a high quality product, developed on time and within budget. How will project managers know when the goals can be achieved?

Goals should be specific, realistic, and measurable. How do you know if you are making progress toward your goal? Marvin Minsky, cofounder of the Artificial Intelligence Laboratory at MIT, formulated the process progress principle as a way to improve the blind trial-and-error search: "Any process of exhaustive search can be greatly reduced if we posses some ways to detect when 'progress' has been made. Then we can trace a path toward a solution, just as a person can climb an unfamiliar hill in the dark—by feeling around, at every step, to find the direction of steepest ascent" [5]. This principle represents a way in which an easy problem can be solved.

What do we do if the problem is really hard to solve? That is when the second statement comes into play: "Goals and Subgoals. The most powerful way we know for discovering how to solve a hard problem is to find a method that splits it into several simpler ones, each of which can be solved separately" [5]. The significance of this statement is that Minsky *formulates the problems in terms of goals.*

The goal should be maintained. If we do not maintain the goal, all of our efforts to solve the problem are wasted. Records of the process followed to solve the problem should be kept to provide information about how to solve a similar problem in the future (historical data collection).

Defining the goal's performance measure (what you will track to measure success) and targets (how much, or how fast success is required) will provide you with criteria against which you can assess the results. For example, my son is in the ninth grade in high school and he is learning mathematics. A target for measuring his math achievement is his "test performance," and a measure of success is that at least 86% of the problems on a test are answered correctly. In software project management, if your goal is to improve the accuracy of software bug descriptions in the software problem reports, the target for measuring is the number of bugs reported and the measure for this target will be 5% of incomplete software problem reports. The measure of success is 95% of problem reports closed. So, the structure is very simple: goal–target–measure (GTM).

Constraints are limiting factors, such as amount of money allocated for a project by the contract and the availability of trained developers. Typically, there are three types of constraint: time, resources, and deliverables. Constraints are conditions we must live with. Resource constraints involve three different areas: budgets, people, and equipment.

Alternatives are the choices available that we can use to minimize the risk associated with not achieving the goal. The management decision process is a mental process. During this process the project manager is trying to connect goals and constraints with possible alternatives to determine the most valuable alternative and come to a decision. The decision arrives during the process of aggregation and quantification of collected information, in which goals and constraints are analyzed and reduced to a number. The project manager has to break the decision scenario into small pieces. This is not a big problem. The difficulty is to identify the potential problem.

You may recall a story about Rumpelstiltskin. Rumpelstiltskin was a dwarf who helped the miller's daughter weave flax into gold in return for a promise that she would give him her firstborn son. Once her son was born, she refused to keep the bargain. Rumpelstiltskin told her that if she could learn his name by midnight of the third day, she could keep the child. At midnight on the third day she told him his name and

Rumpelstiltskin disappeared. Identifying your problem is the first step toward solving it!

First name and analyze the problem in order to state project goals and constraints. It is impossible to eliminate all problems, but we can focus on the current problems and allow the process to grow and mature in order to deal with the problems of the next stage.

Project managers never have any problems naming constraints; unfortunately, they seem to weigh them against goals and alternatives in isolation. Software project management requires close consideration of the goal–constraints–alternatives (GCA) relationships.

If the organization understands this very simple concept, quantifies those three components, and makes decisions based on actual data, not on somebody's gut feeling, there is a very strong possibility that they will achieve Level 2 of CMM in a manageable period of time. They can represent the problems and goals of software project tracking and oversight, software project planning, software subcontract management, requirements management, SQA, and software configuration management in a quantitative way, and make decisions based on factual information.

Decision-making activities and achievement of goals

The quality of your decisions, which makes your organization effective and efficient in the short and long runs in software process improvement, depends on how you develop the software improvement organizational culture. A lot of this depends on an understanding of *why*, *when*, and *how* the information flow changes during the software development life cycle. Each organization implements software process improvement and CMM in different ways. There are no ready-made recipes. Why? Because companies are different and the people who are implementing the processes are different. To implement CMM, looking at the CMM requirements is only the part of the process. You have to look at the people who are doing the actual implementation. They have to decide what is suitable for their particular organization. The direct and bold implementation of the model will lead you to a dead-end after spending a lot of money and wasting a lot of man-hours. Your goal is to improve the software process. Do not get hooked on the CMM levels. The process that you build should be independent of the organizational structure. The definition of the organizational structure should be part of the software process improvement activities. The policies and procedures, which you develop, are part of that activity as well. They help you to build, follow, and improve the process. They form and improve the corporate knowledge of what was implemented and how it was improved. Minsky says, "You might argue that a beaver goes through many steps to build a dam, as does a colony of termites when it builds a complex castle nest. However, these wonderful animals do not learn such accomplishments as individuals but use procedures that have become encoded in their species' genes over millions of years of evolution" [5].

There is a golden rule: Do not get involved in a project that you cannot complete. Do not get involved in a project that you will be ready to give up at the first sign of trouble. To implement CMM, we must create a win–win situation, which supports the reason why we do have to improve the process. The reason should support the long term objective. Therefore, the organization should have long-term vision. Long-term vision and a common goal help to prevent and resolve any conflicts. Conflict usually exists between people who have to contribute to process improvement and the people who commit and lead the process improvement. More questions can be raised: "What is it all for?" "What must I give up for this?" "What is in this for me?"

> *A local busybody who wanted to be rewarded for bringing good news ran to the*
> *Mulla's house one day.*
> *"Nasrudin! Good news!"*
> *"What is it?"*
> *"They are baking cakes next door!"*
> *"What is it for me?"*
> *"But they are going to give you some!"*
> *"What is that to you?"*

The conflict can destroy any process improvement effort, including implementation of CMM. Implementation of CMM can result in personality conflicts. Consider the following typical example of conflict between a software development manager (SDM) and the person responsible for the software process improvement effort, chairman of SEPG.

SDM: "We can't absorb more change, so I'm not going to spend resources I do not have." (This comment means do not mess up our development schedule. Your changes might work, but it will delay project release.)

SEPG: "Efforts to implement improved software development practices within our organization, using CMM as a guideline, have stopped. Evidence of this stoppage includes the following:

- SEPG members have no time to attend meetings or work on developing documented procedures.

- Planning for the next release includes no implementation of requirements management, the very first procedure that the SEPG has documented and provided to the staff.

- The project management responsible for the next product release is not going to implement processes that achieve CMM Level 2."

The SEPG statement means that there is a resistance to change from the mid-management. The SEPG chairman might be thinking, "They do not understand the importance of our push for quality and are trying to throw us back to the stone age."

You can disagree on many issues, except one: You must share the same interests, vision, and goals.

The success of the process improvement effort depends heavily on the strategy of the implementation and the type of goals–subgoals structure (Figure 4.1). This process usually begins with an understanding of the following:

- Where are all the organizational functions performed?

- How are these functions performed together?

- What is the real situation?

These three questions are typically answered by the initial process baseline, and they are the input needed to understand the present situation.

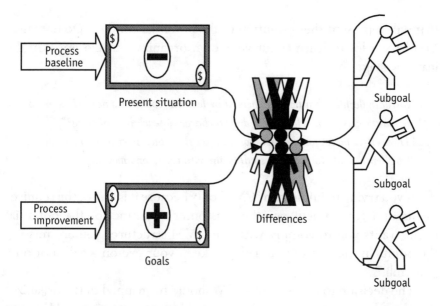

Figure 4.1 Definition of subgoals.

The inputs to the goals are usually the description of the ideal situation, or what you want to achieve over a certain period of time. It can be improvement of the quality of the product, to be certified by the International Organization for Standardization (ISO), or the ability to control the process of software development. At this point, the actual assessment framework or implementation of the model is not important. What is important is the ability of the organization to take the model and adapt it.

The next step is to understand and resolve the differences between the current situation and goal achievement.

- How is the CMM implementation going to affect job functions?

- What problems surrounding the implementation of CMM will we be able to solve?

- Which goals are considered worthy of pursuit?

- What are the methods to reach the goal?

After resolving the differences, you can start to develop the strategy for a successful implementation by developing and prioritizing the subgoals that will represent the resolution of the potential conflict. Do not rush. You have a lot to learn about your own organization. Do not skip the learning stage.

> *Nasrudin decided that he could benefit by learning something new. He went to see master musician. "How much do you charge to teach lute-playing?"*
> *"Three silver pieces for the first month; after that, one silver piece a month."*
> *"Excellent!" said Nasrudin. "I shall begin with the second month."*

If you trying to implement CMM only because it is one of the requirements of a government or other customer's contract or the potential client wants you to comply with the CMM structure, you are missing the point. In this game, you have "to keep your eye on a ball, not on a golf club."

The decision to implement CMM should be mapped to the organizational goal to make a profit. One of the hidden purposes of CMM is to help the organization to manage and make a profit through the effectiveness and efficiency of the organizational processes.

CMM allows and provides a way for management to look at the organization as a whole, not just at the "heroic effort" of one particular individual or group. Measurement of the software development process, and therefore organizational behavior, provides a quantitative way for management to review standardized information in a productive manner. It allows for hard facts and tangible information, which can be discussed during project review meetings. It provides the capability to make meaningful decisions that will satisfy the very important objective of your organization to develop a high-quality product on schedule and within budget, which will lead to profit making.

The available information, as it exists at any given moment, is the basis for the current decision that controls management action. The action or activity changes the level or condition of the software development organization as a system. This is the needed information that is the basis for the decision process. The decision depends on what data are available, what we can get, and what we know how to use.

The majority of companies are overloaded with a lot of different data. This can be very useful for analysis of project performance, but only if we have structured procedures describing how and what data should be considered, analyzed, and interpreted. Of course, there are cases when the data collection process does not exist, or collected data are distorted during the course of a project or simply truncated by the end of the development life cycle.

A typical example of how the lack of collected and analyzed information results in a big decision-making challenge for management is that of deciding whether to release software for integration, beta testing, or customer acceptance testing.

Process management and the measurement process

You cannot develop a quality software product or improve the process without measurements. As Lord Kelvin phrased it: "When you can measure what you are speaking about, and express it in numbers, you know something about it; but when you cannot measure it, when you cannot express it in numbers, your knowledge is of a meager and unsatisfactory kind: it may be the beginning of knowledge, but you have scarcely, in your thoughts, advanced to the stage of science, what ever the matter may be" [6]. When we are trying to use measurements and metrics to analyze the process of software development or separate events that occurred during the development process, it does not really improve the understanding of such. As an event progresses in time the possible state of such an event changes. The term *metrics* is just an abstraction referring to the measurement of the productivity of the process, quality of the product, and predictability of the project. Metrics are useless if they do not represent the right attribute of the process. The set of metrics representing software process attributes, product quality, and project performance predictability should report the status of each phase of product development as well as resources affected by each phase. Process effectiveness and therefore the improvement opportunities should be analyzed through measurements of the product, process, and quality of management. The relationships between the types of measures and general goal are represented in Figure 4.2.

Measures must be analyzed to identify weak aspects of the defined process and to provide feedback to improve the process. This can be a

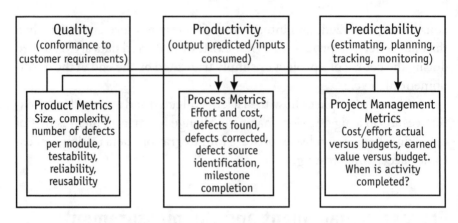

Figure 4.2 Process measurement metrics [7].

process used within the development program (*intra-development process control or improvement*) or within the framework of a database of process definitions, thereby leveraging process improvements across programs and organizations (*institutionalized organizational or inter-development process improvement*) [7].

In spite of the number of suggested very specific software development models, the general definition of the software development process is abstract. An abstraction is created to help us to understand the behavior relevant to the software development organization. Software process improvement or implementation of CMM begins with an understanding of what the process is about.

The process of software development is a process of managing the information flow and information delivery. It is a process of information communication and information representation, not merely code development or application testing.

When we say "measure process," we need to define what we mean. Are we measuring the parameters or the characteristics of the process? What we measure are the indicators of the process, or to be more specific the key *subprocess indicators* representing the specific process steps. (Remember Hora the watchmaker?)

Take a look at Figure 4.3. This figure shows that all measurements are driven by customer requirements of quality and the timeliness of product delivery. The customer satisfaction measure reflects the customer's

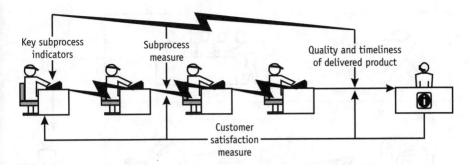

Figure 4.3   Measuring process.

perception of the software product and support services. Measures of quality and timeliness of software product delivery reflect the company's perception not only of the customer's requirements, but of their own requirements as well. Subprocess measures represent the output of subprocesses, and key subprocess indicators represent the output of specific process steps. *The management of the software development process begins with definition of the key subprocess indicators and the output of the subprocess.*

To adopt the preceding proposition, we have to start thinking of the software development process from a systems engineering perspective (Figure 4.4). This perspective is based on the definition of the system, which must consider the existence of a set of subsystem parts and the relationships among them. Therefore, we must define the set of subsystems, that is, a set of intermediate boundaries, and then define how to quantify, estimate, and forecast the conditions that the system imposes on its subsystems. This approach leads us to the system divided into these subsystems: project management and planning, software engineering, software development, and customers. The problem, which is typical for the software development process, is what data should be collected, who should collected it, who will do the data analysis, and, most importantly, how will these actions cure the ineffective process?

To understand the cure for the process, first we have to define the process drivers and how those drivers should be measured and represented, that is, software development process metrics.

Looking at Table 4.1, it is very easy to understand that managing the process refers to managing the rate of change presented by different volatility metrics. There are two major patterns involving change, depending

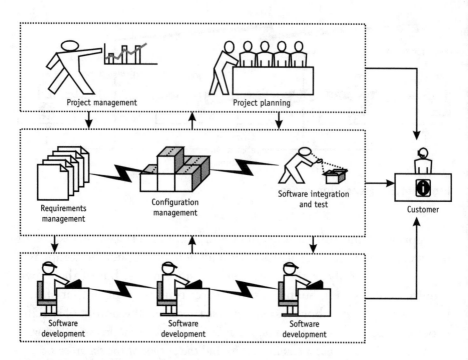

Figure 4.4 Software development process from the systems engineering perspective.

Table 4.1
Process Drivers

Process Drivers	Process Measure	Process Metric
Project management and planning	Time and effort spent Allocation of personnel and frequency of change	Changes between time and effort allocated and time and effort spent Personnel changes
Software engineering	Frequency and distribution of changes in requirements, design units, and software units integrated	Volatility of requirements Volatility of design Volatility of number of software units integrated
Software development	Frequency and changes in SLOC in the configuration system	Volatility of SLOC Software growth over time
Customer satisfaction	Customer satisfaction index	Volatility of the customer satisfaction

on whether the change is rapid or slow—whether it occurs in a day or months. You have to define what is a good change, what makes good process, and how the process reacts to such a positive change.

There are some important questions that should be asked continuously:

- Do we have the ability to respond to change?

- Who is managing the process?

- How is the process tracked?

- What actions should be taken to improve the process?

What do we measure?

There is no point in measuring something or relating one set of measurements to another unless the measurements are applicable to a systematically defined concept. The main consideration in measurement planning is the coordination between the measurement procedure and the concept at which the procedure is aimed. When setting out to measure a variable, we have to look first for the available measure that can meet the requirements. *The variable is data, representing the stage of the process, and not a process attribute that is indexed or reflected by the data.*

Do not waste time developing your own measures. The main idea here is to establish a set of common measuring procedures, so that your software development process knowledge can be built around each subprocess and the relationships among subprocesses. The same procedures can be used for the future, and a developed set of metrics shall be common to a cluster of collected data. For example, let's say you want to understand the adherence to coding standards. You develop a procedure to measure the complexity of the code and the complexity threshold. The complexity flow lets you track and report on project and organizational standards such as lines of code or cyclomatic complexity.

The identification of variables and quantification of the software development life cycle activity maps to the common features of the CMM. The measurements should be part of your development process and described in the documented procedures. Regardless of the measures selected, the procedure should provide a clear picture of the target or threshold and be aimed at the specific key process area.

Let us consider Figure 4.5. Software development standards and procedures define not only the process of the software product development and software life cycle activities, but what process attributes should be measured, what data should be collected, when to collect the data, how data are collected, and who is responsible for data collection. Measured process variables, represented by the collected data, are integrated into the set of software or management metrics. The correlated set of metrics, called *indicators,* points to the deficiencies of the development process and potential improvement opportunities. Identification of the process improvement opportunities, in return, can point to the changes in organizational standards and procedures. Procedures should be continuously improved in order to raise the threshold of the organizational standards to the next, higher level. This very simple concept describes the dynamics of the measurement process and the importance of metrics, which can influence the whole software process improvement effort, or CMM implementation. This concept can help you to move from one level to another on a maturity scale.

Different events, taking place during the software development process, differ from one another by the number of different environmental conditions and by qualifying factors in terms of how the conditions were perceived. The process of selection of the qualifying factors can be represented by several variables. Therefore, without correlation and cross-referencing of information that can represent those factors with a specific goal and meaning, we are just selecting one variable from many possibilities. For instance, the complexity of software modules does not allow you to test the product to its full extent; one result is unexpected software failures. Correlation of these two measurements (complexity and software failures) cannot be directly observed, but it is very clear how they relate to each other.

In the most general term, the process of software development has many meanings. When applied to specifics, it may be interpreted as interaction between the software life-cycle development and the business cycle, computer components, and people. The instrumental value is in pursuing a long-range company goal. The two fundamental strategies in process analysis are the experimental and co-relational strategies.

Standards and
procedures

Software life
cycle activities

Issues analysis and
process improvement
opportunities

Indicators

Metrics

Measurements

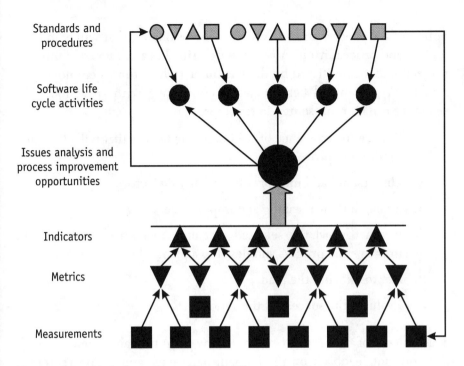

Figure 4.5   Links between software life cycle and measurements.

The crucial difference between the experimental and the co-relational approaches is evidenced by the type of question asked before analysis begins. The experimental analyst asks: "Does the process tend to react in a particular way to the changed conditions?" The co-relational analyst asks: "Does the subprocess whose behavior shows a lot of a particular tendency also have a lot of another tendency?" Simply put, the experimental approach studies the effect of an independent variable, a condition usually manipulated by the experimenter. The fundamental requirement of this approach is that every other condition that might affect the variable being studied and the dependent variable are expected to co-vary with independent conditions. The co-relational approach studies subprocesses as they are. In such studies the goal is to estimate the range of variables [8].

The key point is this: *Always take into account what is influencing your process, otherwise you will not be able to draw the objective conclusion.*

Process behavior is specified by a succession of events and qualifying factors and the time interval between them. If we apply the general notion of the process and analyze the process phases, that will help us to understand process itself. A *process* is described as a sequence of internal project activities initiated by the customer (which forces employees to modify organizational behavior) and concluding with an action. The sequence can be represented in six steps.

1. Realize the existence of the qualifying factors that will affect and modify the process.

2. Understand and interpret the qualifying factors.

3. Evaluate their meaning and importance.

4. Reach toward the selected meaning; make a commitment to improve the process and develop a plan.

5. Act to execute the plan.

6. Evaluate the success of the action.

This concept of a general process has many potential values, one of which is a constant feedback on the human experience and action required; another is a framework for organizing the many kinds of variables. The variables we want to consider refer to aspects of phases of the process. Consideration should be given to establishing sufficient methodology and terminology so that variables will have the same meaning to everyone [8].

This concept of the general process can be interpreted as the IDEAL model developed by the SEI. You can find a description of the model in *The Capability Maturity Model: Guidelines for Improving the Software Process* [4]. IDEAL is an acronym that represents the five stages of software process improvement cycle.

1. *Initiating:* Stimulate improvement, set and establish sponsorship, and establish improvement infrastructure.

2. *Diagnosing:* Appraise and characterize current practice, develop recommendations, and document phase results.

3. *Establishing:* Set strategy and priorities, establish process action team, and plan actions.

4. *Acting:* Define processes and measures; plan and execute pilots; plan, execute, and track installations.

5. *Leveraging:* Document and analyze lessons, and revise organizational approach.

This framework describes the necessary phases of activity and resources needed for successful process improvement efforts. Tables 4.2 shows us how it corresponds to the general process description presented earlier.

Until now, industry has been too engaged in the development of methodologies to think about measurements. It is a time to start putting together methodologies and measurements.

The specifics and informational content vary from project to project, and from one organization to another. Before any models for process improvement are considered for implementation, some very important steps should be taken.

- Critical business issues, specific to your organization, should be identified.

- Identify existing organizational key processes.

- Document and analyze the existing processes.

- Set a goal for improvement. What do you expect from process improvement?

- Establish the measurement procedures.

Table 4.2
Comparison of the General Processes and IDEAL Model

General Process	IDEAL
Realize the existence of the qualifying factors	Initiating
Understand and interpret the qualifying factors	Diagnosing
Evaluate their meaning and importance	Diagnosing
Reaching to its meaning	Establishing
Make a commitment to improve the process and develop a plan	Establishing
Acting to execute plan	Acting
Evaluating success of action	Leveraging

By taking these steps you will place process improvement activities in the context of your strategy and structure. These steps will help you to determine the variety of informational flow activities—from the documentation work flow to the determination to the cost of the current process. If you decide to implement CMM, it will help you to reorganize policies and procedures and to identify required changes to make project activities more effective.

The process itself has several stages or phases. It is initiated by external requirements. The outside requirements are registered, perceived, and interpreted. We consider here the relationships between the different parts of the process and how to describe the behavior of individual subprocesses. To do that variables should be identified. What are and how do we define process variables? A process variable is a measurable *quantity*, which at every instant has a definite numerical value. A process variable is also a *quality* in that the behavior of the processes differ. These two variables (quantity and quality) are related to the management of any process. The quality and quantity variables should be understood and balanced carefully [8].

It is impossible to measure a variable if we cannot describe it. The measurement goal has to be defined and communicated to the people involved in software development.

CMM tries to encapsulate both process variables in common features, but it emphasizes primarily the qualitative part of the model. The quantitative part, called measurements and verifications, is usually left alone until an organization starts thinking about Level 4. People are sometimes surprised to learn that a measurement is a part of every KPA at every maturity level.

Selecting information

The main requirement of CMM in managing the software development life cycle should be supported by a "committed" management system that supports software process improvement. In the process of improvement, the primitive events are defined, and a bottom-up approach is used for their generalization.

What are the primitive events? How do we select what information to collect and measure? What are the components of the measurement procedure? In his book *Philosophical Foundation of Physics,* R. Carnal writes: "Of course all our knowledge has its origins in singular statements—the particular observations of particular individuals. One of the big perplexing questions in the philosophy of science is how we are able to go from such singular statements to the assertion of universal laws" [9].

Measured information is a reflection of the event or process. Measurement-related information is created inside a certain system or process and exists in some tangible form. Information is created under the influence of outside events and exists independently from the event that generated such information. The critical role or meaning of information is its correspondence to the event or process. The meaning and the semantic content of the measurement-related information is an isomorphic reflection of the outside event.

If we have both an event or process in different states and the information described in different symbols, we can correlate the elements of those symbols to particular domains. That is, we can apply the meaning of every symbol, which will correspond to the one of the states of the process.

The selection of the right information is a selection of one symbol or element from the many possible choices. That selection process will be determined by the event that correlates to the respective information. The system, where the information resides, provides the conditions for the information's existence. We can model the process because of the isomorphism of different events related to a process. The isomorphic process model reflects the real process and allows us to analyze its behavior in a wide range of constantly changing conditions. The most important aspect in the nature of information is that information represents many different states of the process. The information about many different conditions of the process can be measured, cross-referenced, correlated, and translated with each other [8].

The existence of information representing process events allows us to generate certain actions. Combined with other information, it can create new information, which can carry another meaning and potentially generate another action or event. There is a link between information and event, and a correlation between them exists in the boundaries specified by the degree of the details available for the event.

Project model

Within each project boundary, the basic building block is the feedback loop. The dynamic behavior of the project is generated by feedback. The feedback loop is a path that integrates decision, action, state of the project, and information about the project, with the path returning to the decision level (Figure 4.6).

A decision process is one that controls any project action. Whatever the nature of the decision process, it is always integrated in a feedback loop. The feedback loop delivers a response about the project's condition to the project manager. The decision is based on that project information. The management decision controls and creates an action that influences the state of the project. New incoming information from the project or the outside environment modifies the decision flow. The feedback loop is a structural component of the project management process. *Every project management decision made occurs inside of the feedback loop. The decision controls all action, which changes the state of the project, which influences the decision* [10].

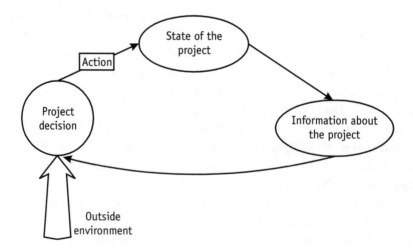

Figure 4.6 Feedback and project decision.

The feedback loop structure should be part of any management decision-making process. Let us look at it one more time and summarize:

- It presents the results of a past action so to guide present decisions.

- The action represents the flow of project activities controlled by the decision.

- The action is based on available information and controls the decision.

- The state of the project alters the actions.

- The state of the project is the true condition of the project and is the source of information about the project.

- The state of the project is the present condition of the project. It is the result of all of the past decisions and represents the history of all past actions.

- Information about the present decisions and actions do not tell us anything about the state of the project.

- Delay in collecting data can cause the data to be inaccurate so they do not represent the true state of the project.

- Decisions made change the information on which they are based.

- The present state of the project is not determined by the present actions.

There are two fundamental types of variables within the feedback loop or the substructure of the feedback loop: condition variables and the action variables. Both are important. Condition variables describe the state of the project at any particular time. They integrate and represent the results of actions within the project [10].

Action variables tell how fast the state of the project changes, the volatility of the events. Action variables are not determined by the present value of the condition variables, the slope of the condition variable (such as number of SLOCs) developed over time (number/time). The action variable does not depend on its own past value, or the time interval between computations, but only on the changed values of the condition variable. *The state of a project and rate of change make up the informational feed-back loop substructure. Condition variables integrate the results of project action. They create informational flow continuity between points in time. The rates of information flow do not determine the present state of a project, merely the quickness with which the state is changing* [10].

The condition variables feed information to the action variables and, in return, action variables cause changes only in state variables. The condition variables carry the continuity of the project-related information from the past to the present. Condition variables contain all of the past and present history of the project. If the condition values are known, the rates of change (action variables) can be calculated.

Let us relate this theoretical exercise to our case. The *condition variables* are the data sets (point-in-time data) or numbers you collect by measuring the software development life cycle: requirements number, software size, code complexity, personnel, number of faults, number of test cases executed. The *action variables* are the computed numbers that identify the rate of change, or trends such as requirements stability, software volatility, fault density, and fault intensity [10].

The condition and action variables are represented by the metrics. The only purpose of metrics is to represent information that accompanies the numbers. Metrics are not isolated things. They are data sets used to understand, as a total picture, the project issues that require decisions to be made. Most metrics are more meaningful when presented as trend data instead of point-in-time data.

Good organizations compute meaningful metrics as a matter of course, because it helps them to control processes and make meaningful decisions. They use metrics as a tool to control and improve their technical efforts and costs. Some organizations consider metrics to be a necessary evil that increases the costs of overhead.

Figure 4.7 shows the integration of the informational structure of the project management system into the CMM structure in a number of steps.

1. The organizational environment triggers appropriate actions at appropriate times.

2. Project management is concerned with three main issues: cost, schedule, and quality.

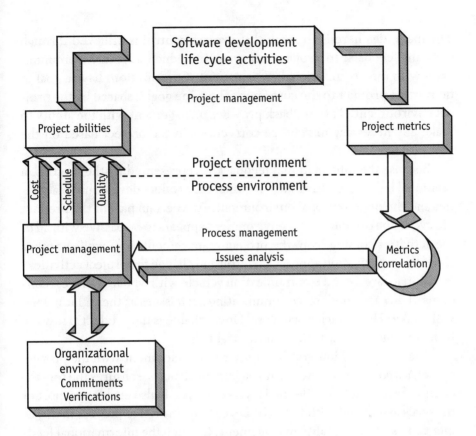

Figure 4.7   Integration of a project's informational structure into CMM.

3. People involved in a project should have the ability to develop the product.

4. Product development activities are controlled and coordinated by management.

5. The control of the project's activities is accomplished by the project metrics.

6. Project metrics are correlated in order to identify the potential effect on a project.

7. Potential problems are identified and a decision is made to make a midcourse correction.

The main idea here is to show that project control is achieved through constant feedback to project management, which in return communicates with the organizational environment. Organizations have a goal to deliver the product to the customer. The same goal is shared by the project environment. The feedback provides management with the ability to make any necessary midcourse corrections in the project based on the past performance.

Because the informational feedback is represented by the metrics, a relational balance is established between the product development activities and the organizational environment. At a certain part of the product life cycle, the organizational environment appears to be passive with all of the activities coming from the project management side, while at other times the organization appears to step in and change the project activities.

Metrics are a good communication vehicle with which to address concerns. They are good for communicating such issues as these: How long will it take? How much it will cost? How reliable is the product? How big is the product? What is the commercial risk?

The concept of integration of metrics development with the process of metrics correlation into the management structure ensures the togetherness of repeatable and defined levels of KPAs. It also enables support of the goals associated with KPAs of Level 4 (quantitative process management and software quality management) through the informational feedback loop supported by the same concept.

Confusion can arise between record keeping and a goal-oriented organizational performance. There is a relationship between internal project goals and organizational goals, which should be coordinated.

The implementation of such complex structures as CMM, in which the overall goal is to achieve the desired Level 5, can be maintained by means of organized subgoals that can be pursued simultaneously. The presented project and process structure allows a project to achieve and maintain the dynamic project and process stability in relation to the project and process environment.

No model, CMM included, will ever represent reality. The purpose of CMM is to provide information that can be communicated clearly and to clarify our knowledge and our insights into the project and process.

Of course, the information collected about the project is not perfect. There is no such thing in the physical or social sciences as perfect information, but dealing with information of intermediate quality is better than no information at all. CMM is a management model. It represents people, their decisions, and their reaction to the pressure of the organizational environment. We have to keep in mind the relative nature of the model, rather than absolute measures, as represented by the required metrics. The representation cannot be perfect. It should serve the organization, however, in allowing management to see the consequences of decisions made, right or wrong. The success of CMM implementation will pave the way toward software process improvement and subsequently the accuracy with which we can represent the reality.

When we reduce CMM to a set of software metrics, when its underlying assumptions can be presented and examined, when it can be communicated to management and practitioners, and when we correlate metric information into indicators to determine the behavior of the process of producing the software, then we can reasonably hope to understand our project environment better. That practice will help us comprehend and communicate CMM, as well as solve many problems related to project and organizational environments, and can be directed toward organizational goals, easier communication, and improved project management.

We may call the process of step-by-step KPA representation via metrics and indicators the "metrification" of CMM. The metrification technique is used as a process simulation and provides a very inexpensive way to obtain useful information about the dynamics of the software development process. It also provides valuable insight into project management issues.

Measurement concepts

How many times have you asked yourselves this question?: "Why does management want us to play that metric game and waste our time displaying charts on the walls? Do the measurements and metrics we are using have some substance that reflects the actual project situation?" To understand the nature of this question, let's return to our roots again.

Believe it or not, the first project performance evaluation practice goes back to the biblical age. Do you remember the story of Gideon in the

Book of Judges? Gideon selected his group of warriors for a special mission based on two tests. The first test was based on the motivation of the warrior. Those who did not want to participate were allowed to leave. For the second test, they had to drink from a body of water. Those who put their heads down to drink the water were rejected, but those who brought water up to their mouths in their hands were selected for the mission, because they supposedly were more alert and watchful [8].

By looking at this example, we can outline four main concepts.

1. Set a goal (to win the battle).

2. Observe the condition of the environment (the availability of the body of water).

3. Develop a way to identify possible discrepancy between the stated goal and observed future performance (how warriors drink the water).

4. Define on what to base the decision of selecting the right warrior (the performance test).

There is another way to look at this example, which describes how the available information is used to generate decisions.

We can transform this example into the project environment.

1. A goal;

2. An observed condition of the project;

3. A way to express the difference between the goal and observed condition;

4. A declaration of how an action is chosen based on this difference.

These four items are related, and the rate of change equation can be presented as follows: *Deviation From the Goal = (Desired Goal − Observed Condition).* (Do you remember planned versus actual metrics?)

Now let us add the time component to the preceding equation: *Rate of Change = (Desired Goal − Observed Condition) / Time.* We just came to the conclusion that the rate of change is a very important management indicator that allows deviation from the project or process goals to be managed.

Therefore, a very important measurement principle is revealed: Compare the goal with the project condition to detect a discrepancy. Use the discrepancy to guide the action. This measurement principle helps to identify the goal quantitatively, define quantitatively how productive you are in achieving the goal, and identify how to measure the deviation in goal achievements.

The structure of CMM helps and guides us in organizing information through the activities of the KPAs. If we know the pattern, we can successfully interpret the incoming data. The pattern is not necessarily one of the suggested software development life cycle models. The pattern is software development phases and activities.

References

[1] Wilson, J. W., "The Growth of a Company: A Psychological Study," *Advanced Management Journal,* 1966, p. 43.

[2] Corning, P.A., *The Synergism Hypothesis,* New York: Mc-Graw Hill, 1983.

[3] Simon, H. A., "Architecture of Complexity," General Systems 10, 1965, 65–66.

[4] Paulk, M. C., et al.,*The Capability Maturity Model: Guidelines for Improving the Software Process,* Reading, MA: Addison-Wesley, 1995.

[5] Minsky, M., *The Society of Mind,* New York: Simon and Schuster, 1988

[6] Kaplan, A. *The Conduct of Inquiry: Methodology for Behavioral Science,* San Francisco: Chandler, 1964, p. 172.

[7] Hart, H., et al., "STARS Process Concept Summary," *TRI-Ada Conference Proceedings,* Orlando, Florida, November 1992.

[8] Fiske, D., *Measuring the Concepts of Personality,* Chicago: Aldine Publishing Company, 1971

[9] Carnal, R., *Philosophical Foundation of Physics.*

[10] Forester, J. W., *Principles of Systems,* Cambridge, MA: MIT Press.

5

Connecting Measurements to CMM Key Process Areas

We look at it and do not see it.

Lao-tzu, sixth century B.C.

Connecting the software development life cycle and software project management

An organization produces its product and supports its customers through cross-functional business processes, not individual functions. If the organization has the ability to meet a customer's present and future needs, it means that organization manages cross-functional processes and stays competitive. Cross-functional processes are not obvious, not easily detectable, and not easily understood.

CMM tries to help to identify, structure, manage, and improve cross-functional processes by presenting 18 KPAs.

Let us now develop a framework, a type of skeleton, for software product development (Figure 5.1). The first frame, which is the default frame, is a software development life cycle. This frame is a very general frame and not attached to any specific product. For any product, the software development organization is going through the full cycle from the software requirements definition to product maintenance and support. The success of how this frame is applied represents and depends solely on the past organizational experience with developing software products and the skill of the software engineers.

The second frame of Figure 5.1 is the frame of project management. This frame has great significance because this frame deals with important management issues such as costs, scheduling, and quality. This frame is used for understanding and predicting what may happen with the project and for preventing adverse situations when expectations are not met.

These two frames represent everything that is pertinent to the project. They represent the processes of software development and project management. Are they connected? Of course they are, you might say. But if project management is so well connected to the software development life cycle, why are most actions of project managers reactive, rather than proactive?

In a typical software development organization, the two frames are attached only superficially, in spite of active communication and interaction between them all the time. To learn more about project status, we have to combine two different parts of the product development process. To understand the proper meaning, we have to establish a connection between the project management structure and the software development life cycle so that those parts will communicate and transmit information continuously. It is like driving a car in that you establish a

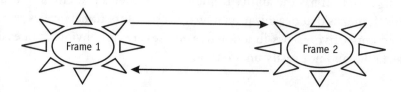

Figure 5.1 Framework for software product development.

connection between the car and a road. Consider this example from Marvin Minsky's book, *The Society of Mind*: "Jack drove from Boston to New York on the turnpike with Mary" [1]. As soon you hear such a statement, parts of your mind become engaged with the types of concerns related to driving (Table 5.1). "These concerns and roles seem so important that every language has developed special word-forms or grammatical construction of them. How do we know who drove the car? We know that it's Jack—because the Actor comes before the verb. How do we know a car was involved? Because that is default Vehicle for drive. When did it happen? In the past—because the verb drive has the form drove, etc." [1].

Whenever we consider the action, such as moving from one place to another, we almost always have particular concerns like these: Where does the action start? Where does it end? What instrument is used? What is the purpose or goal? What are its effects? What difference will it make? Minsky represented these questions with a simple diagram (Figure 5.2). If you are involved in software project management, you immediately recognize that the same issues recur: what, when, how, why, and who. Those are common features of our mind.

In 1975, Roger Schenk in his book *Conceptual Information Processing* introduced the concept of *trans-frames* [2]. A trans-frame is a type of frame that is centered around the path or route between two situations,

Table 5.1
Concerns and Roles [1]

Role	Concern	Role	Concern
Origin	The initial state	Destination	The final state
Action	What act was done	Actor	Who caused it
Difference	What was changed	Cause	What made the change
Recipient	Who was affected	Method	How it was done
Motive	Why it was done	Obstacle	What was the problem
Trajectory	The selected path	Instrument	What tools were used
Object	What was affected	Vehicle	What vehicle was used
Time	When it happened	Place	Where it occurred

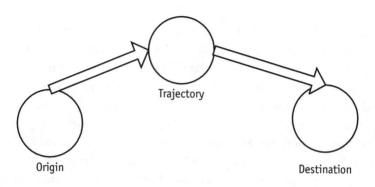

Figure 5.2 Minsky's diagram [1].

"before" and "after." This path represents the action or activity to go from one state of the informational process to another.

To maintain that activity, the information should flow continuously and be exchanged all the time. Look at Figure 5.3. There are four bubbles, which represent the concept of general software development in a traditional sense. Four main functions were traditionally performed in a software organization: requirement definition and software design, project planning and estimation, software production (coding, testing, and integration), and a final step that integrates those three areas together through the organizational and management philosophies.

Inserting the common features of CMM into the bubbles of Figure 5.3 provides us with a connecting link between the software development life cycle and software project management. This link helps us navigate the implementation of the software product by building necessary abilities to perform and monitor the activities performed. At the same time, it will provide management control of the project using a standardized structure of measurement and verification (what, when, why, how, and who).

Each link in Figure 5.4 represents the informational path of the trans-frame, as mentioned earlier. It links the project business strategy to the action of software development. The common features of the KPAs of CMM provide such linkage. They provide the structure and support two-way communication via measurements and metrics.

Let us review the functions of the CMM's common features. It is very important to understand the processes variables that we are going to measure, correlate, and analyze.

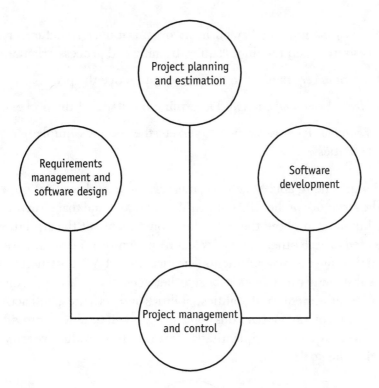

Figure 5.3 Traditional representation of software development.

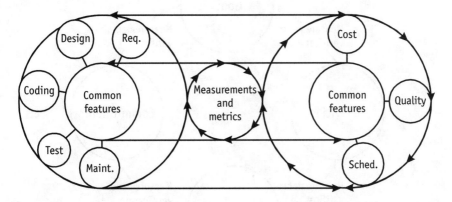

Figure 5.4 Integrating the software development and project management processes.

- *Commitment to perform:* Support the goals, establish policies and procedures, establish leadership.

- *Ability to perform:* Establish an organizational structure, reflect resources and funding, require training and process orientation.

- *Activities performed:* Plan the process, practice the process.

- *Measurement and analysis:* Determine the status of the process.

- *Verifying implementation:* Oversee the process implementation activities.

Commitment, ability, activity, measurement, and verification represent the structure of the KPAs of CMM. To understand that structure, we should understand how the individual components of the structure are connected to each other. It is very clear from Figure 5.5 that they are connected through the measurements–verification (M-V) substructure. The M-V substructure provides a bridge between the goals and commitments, commitments and abilities, abilities and activities, and activities and goals. If you understand this concept, you will be able to provide the answer to this question in quantitative terms: "How productive are you in achieving the goal?"

Figure 5.5   M-V connections of the common features.

Connecting key process areas to the environment

The environment in which a software product is developed is three dimensional and has three components: the organizational, project management, and product development environments (Figure 5.6).

These three environments of a software product are related to each other and linked to the KPAs. They are environments, but CMM calls them process categories. As Paulk pointed out in *The Capability Maturity Model: Guidelines for Improving the Software Process,*

> One of the most controversial decisions in developing the CMM was defining key process areas to reside at a single maturity level. The primary reason for this decision was to simplify the presentation of how to achieve the next maturity level. Separating out the issues specific to achieving the maturity level clarified the understanding of what was needed to achieve a maturity level. Key process areas are not processes, as this controversy highlights. A process changes over time and hopefully matures. A process is dynamic. A key process area describes essential attributes (i.e., key practices of a process) when that process is fully realized. A key process area is static; it describes a process at a high level of abstraction and does not tell how the process is performed [3].

In Table 5.2 we try to group the KPAs into categories that represent the three environments mentioned earlier: project management, product development, and organizational, using CMM guidelines.

Figure 5.6 The three components of a software product.

Table 5.2
KPAs Grouped According to the Three Environments of a Software Product

Project Management Environment			
Repeatable	**Defined**	**Managed**	**Optimized**
Software project planning	Integrated software management	Quantitative process management	—
Software project tracking and oversight	—	—	—
Product Development Environment			
Repeatable	**Defined**	**Managed**	**Optimized**
Requirements management	Software product engineering	Software quality management	Defect prevention
Software configuration management	Intergroup coordination	—	—
Software subcontract management	Peer review	—	—
Organizational Environment			
Repeatable	**Defined**	**Managed**	**Optimized**
Software quality assurance	Organizational process definition	—	Technology change management
—	Organizational process focus	—	Process change management
—	Training program	—	—

In the next step, we represent the project, product, and organizational environments in three-dimensional space. We call this space the *process environment space* (Figure 5.7). This is the space where the process

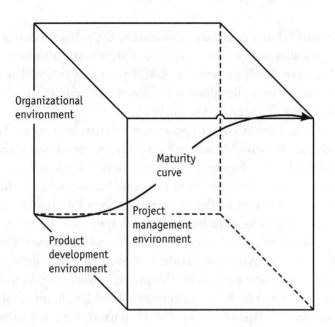

Figure 5.7 The environmental space.

categories mature. This is the space where the action starts and ends. This is the space where goals are accomplished and procedures are implemented. In this space, you are moving from an immature software development organization to the final state of controlling your destiny.

It is only a matter of time before the organization starts thinking about process improvement.

> *A man called, wanting to borrow a rope. "You cannot have it," said Nasrudin.*
> *"Why not?"*
> *"Because it is in use."*
> *"But I can see it just lying there, on the ground!"*
> *"That's right: that's use."*
> *"How long will it stay in use like that, Mulla?"*
> *"Until such time as I feel that I want to lend it out," said Nasrudin.*

If you take a look at Figure 5.7, it is quite a journey to climb from the bottom of the curve to our destination at the top of the curve. The curve inside the environmental space represents the trajectory or the path that you will follow as an organization to mature the software processes. We call this path a *maturity curve*. The maturity curve, although ideally a straight line, can never be straight. CMM provides you with a structure for the maturity curve, but does not tell you how to navigate in the environmental space and stay on the curve.

The software improvement process is a dynamic process. To understand its dynamics, which is shown every day, we need to understand the concept of the *S-curve* (Figure 5.8). The S-curve is a graph that represents the relationship between the effort the organization puts into improving the process and the results the organization gets for that investment of effort. It is called an S-curve because it is shaped like the letter *S*.

In general shape, the S-curve ranges fall and then rise. "Many functions will depict this type of behavior, but one that is interesting and convenient is the cumulative frequency function, known as *ogilvy* in statistics. Any *ogilvy* is confined to the range between 0 and 1.0, in terms of relative, and not absolute, frequency. The general pattern for a continuous variable is an S-shaped curve" [4].

Initially, when process improvement starts, progress is very slow. Then, when the organization gains knowledge of implementation and creates the necessary infrastructure to support process improvement, you can observe significant progress. Finally, as more effort is put into

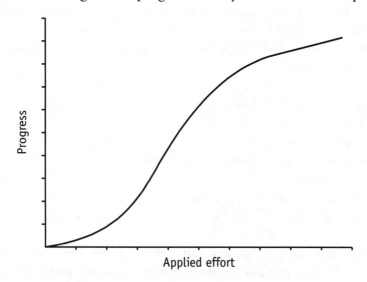

Figure 5.8   The S-curve.

process improvement, it becomes more difficult and expensive to make improvement progress. The risk of implementing unneeded changes is increased, and there is a possibility that development costs will increase because of the chance that more process R&D will be needed, rather than product R&D.

It is not the time that helps you to clime the curve, but the effort applied. The effort applied is to plan, manage, and control.

All 18 KPAs reveal the same philosophy. The project and process should be planned (P), controlled (C), and managed (M): PCM.

Let us build a matrix that will be able to provide guidance in the formulation of the software process improvement objectives. This matrix will focus on project and process, the two variables from which software process improvement objectives and implementation of CMM are drawn.

By positioning the maturity curve on the matrix (Figure 5.9), you can define a strategy of software process improvement implementation.

- 1–2: Planning of the process and project begins. Project control begins.

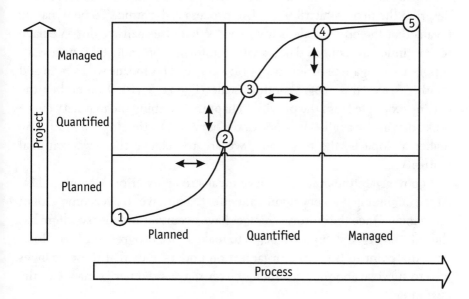

Figure 5.9 Software process and project improvement matrix.

- 2–3: Begin the process and project quantification stage.

- 3–4: Control the process and manage the project.

- 4–5: Manage the process and project (continuous process improvement).

By positioning your response from the maturity questionnaire on a maturity curve, you can evaluate your position on the curve and develop a strategy for improvement.

Do not jump on the CMM implementation bandwagon immediately. Try to understand what informational paths you already have established and use them. Do not rush to implement CMM and do not become hooked on CMM levels. Your goal is continuous software process improvement, and in order to stay competitive, the business and technical objectives of your organization should be aligned.

The maturity curve

As we already know, the environmental space is composed of KPAs that describe the process attributes. The process is dynamic. To be dynamic means that the effort scale is involved. What else shall we do? We have to continuously collect data, analyze information, and take necessary actions to navigate in order to stay on a curve. This means we have to add another scale, the progress-effort scale (Figure 5.10). Remember the driving example from the previous chapter? Climbing the maturity curve is like driving up a hill. The slope of the curve is like the slope of a hill. The higher a slope is, the more able we are to achieve the organizational maturity.

To navigate the maturity curve means to apply effort (Figure 5.11). At the beginning it is very significant effort. You have to overcome a lot of resistance. Once the cultural changes have occurred and the paradigm has shifted, the organization will begin to make more progress for less effort. At some point in time, the organization understands that these changes lead to survival and they can then deliver the desired performance to the customer.

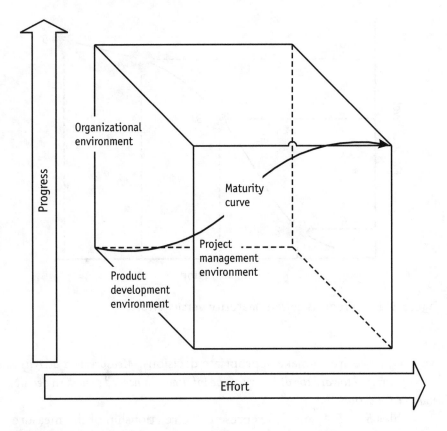

Figure 5.10 Adding the progress-effort scale.

Where we are on a curve is the result of our effort applied to improve the software processes, to change organizational culture, and to keep software projects under control. There is one condition attached: *The processes you implement should be independent of the organizational structure.*

Connecting key process areas and measurements

Let us build a set of tables that connect KPAs and measurement activities. What is the measurement activity? Usually we have something specific in mind when we are involved in measuring. It can be the outside temperature or the number of miles to commute to work. This is the information

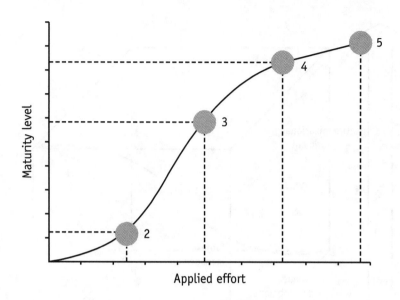

Figure 5.11   Progress toward maturity versus effort.

we need if we are to make appropriate decisions. *Measurement activity is activity directed toward the discovery of the information needed to make a decision and to take action.*

Tables 5.3, 5.4, and 5.5 represent the relationship of the measurement activities to KPAs in the environmental space. These tables can help you build a strategy for CMM implementation.

Defining indicators and issues

A project manager is a person who allocates resources and regulates the activity of a software project. In many cases the software project manager simply adjusts and adapts himself or herself to the company environment and the traditionally accepted way of managing the project. The reason why is easy to explain: pressure.

Project management is overwhelmed with schedule pressure, management pressure, time-to-market pressure, and other pressures. Pressure dominates a project, and, on top of that, there is no effective way to interpret the available project information and interrelate it with past experience without an organizational structure in place. Without

Table 5.3
Product Development and Project Management

	SPP	SPTO	ISM	QPM
RM	Tracking the status and volatility of allocated requirements, summarized by categories. Tracking the changes to the original cost and schedule estimates due to software requirements changes, and impact on projected cost.			
SCM	Tracking of milestones for SCM activities compared to the plan, effort completed software development volatility, and change requests processed.			
SSM	Tracking cost and progress of subcontractor activities and compare to the plan.			
SPE	Requirements are traced across the life cycle; proposed changes and problem reports are analyzed and traced to the source though the development life cycle.			
IC	Tracking effort and resources expended to support other engineering groups. Tracking the schedule and milestone completion dates to coordinate activities of different engineering groups.			
PR	Number of reviews performed compared to the plans. Effort expended on peer reviews compared to the plan. Efficiency of the peer review process.			
SQM	Effort expended over time to manage software project quality, compared to the plan. Software reliability measures. Prediction of software defects. Tracking the cost of achieving the quality goal.			
DP	Number and severity of defects found in software code. Tracking the defect density, intensity, and rate of closure. Cost of defect prevention activities.			

Table 5.4
Organization and Project Management

	SPP	SPTO	ISM	QPM
SQA	Completion of milestones and cost tracking for the SQA activities compared to the plan.			
OPD	Organization's software process database contains historical and actual information about past and present projects: estimates of size, effort, costs, and productivity.			
OPF	Tracking resources expended.			
TP	Progress against training plans. Actual skills available against projected skills.			
TCM	Effectiveness of new technology implemented compared to the goal.			
PCM	Tracking process performance and compare to the predefined limits.			

Table 5.5
Organization and Product Development

	RM	SCM	SSM	SPE	IC	PR	SQM	DP
SQA	Product status and activities review compared to plan, number of product audits and reviews available compared to the SQA planned activities.							
OPD	Organization's software process database contains historical information such as quality measurements, reliability data, peer review coverage.							
OPF	Definition of quality measures.							
TP	Number of training waivers approved over time. Effectiveness of training.							
TCM	Impact of new technology on a software project, tracked over time.							
PCM	Process attribute measurements that relate to the indicators of software process development performance and customer satisfaction.							

structure, a project manager's knowledge is just a collection of observations, practices, and conflicting information. Project issues become major problems. At the same time, the process of managing and controlling project issues is concerned with how to select the decision criteria, which can be used in support of the management philosophies and techniques for the software development project. This problem can be resolved with KPA-related procedures, which are developed from the process descriptions to provide proof of project progress to the management. A good example here would be a set of metrics showing the volatility of process and quality of the product and a matrix showing the traceability of the requirements to the completed test cases. Using this methodology, we are able to manage the interdependencies between subprocesses or trend management.

Let's look at an example of trend analysis, which can help you structure your future measurement activities.

- *Function-based volatility trends:* Function size, function growth, function change density;

- *Data activity trends:* Growth of code, changes in code, rework of code;

■ *Trend activity:* Trend toward growth of code, trend of changes in code, trend toward rework of code.

What are the issues that project manager constantly face? Two major factors increase the risk associated with software development.

1. Project complexity has a strong effect on uncertainty of project outcome.

2. Project size is another important factor. As size increases, the interdependencies among various elements of software grow rapidly.

In 1993, U.S. the Army published a *Streamlined Integrated Software Metrics Approach Guidebook* (SISMA) [5]. The SISMA guidebook identified common software management issues and grouped them into three categories (Table 5.6).

1. Resource issues;

2. Progress issues;

3. Quality issues.

Resource issues deal with resource planning, monitoring, and allocation. Progress issues focus on the current status of a project and projections of future performance. Quality issues bring attention to the quality of the product.

The effect of project management actions cannot be measured directly. It should be something that allows insight into a particular issue and provides feedback regarding management actions. That something should have a structure represented by either graphs or tables or both. That something is called an *indicator*. *Indicator* is a convenient word used merely to mean something that points to something else.

Jerome Brunner emphasized the importance of structure: "Grasping the structure of the subject is understanding it in a way that permits many other things to be related to it meaningfully. To learn structure, in short, is to learn how thing are related" [6].

What does this mean to us? It means that the individual software metric represents a measurable data point and provides a structure of

Table 5.6

Common Software Management Issues

Resource Issues
Cost/budget
Host computer resource utilization
Target computer resource utilization
Personnel/staffing
Progress Issues
Development progress
Test progress
Incremental release content
Milestone completion
Software growth
Productivity
Quality Issues
Stability
Design structure
Test readiness
Error profiles
ADA usage (quality of the code produced)

measurements. Software metrics can be used as a tool to determine and predict the progress toward specific software development goals. The indicator is a tool to correlate metrics in order to identify issues and prevent potential problems associated with the project's goal achievement. For example, if a new estimate prepared during the software design phase represents a significant increase over estimates prepared during the software requirements analysis phase, we may say that this indicates a potential problem with the schedule implementation. If the requirements are volatile during the software development process, it indicates that the schedule will be impacted as well.

If software metrics are integrated into the project management process, they will act as process indicators, and metrics correlation will be able to provide meaningful information about project issues, identify potential problems, and allow early decisions about correction activities. Correlated metrics provide quantitative information in support of management decision making. Therefore, we can formulate this basic concept: *Indicators are the measured variables that establish a relationship between metrics and issues.*

Let us assume that we are in the design phase of a project. The issue that we are concerned with is the growth and stability of the requirements. The indicator, which will point us in the right direction, is the size and stability of the requirements. Growth in the number of requirements indicates additional work, volatility in the project, and poorly defined requirements. This important question should be answered: Are the number of requirements changes large relative to the total number of requirements? Why it is important to ask such a question? Because requirements volatility after software design is completed will result in scheduling problems. The purpose of such an indicator is to identify the areas where changes are occurring and to determine if the milestone performance and effort allocation estimates have been adjusted to accommodate the changes.

Very simple requirements stability metrics can be a starting point for gathering information. Let's next take a look at the issue analysis process.

"*Could you measure the diameter of the globe?*"
"*No that I could not, sir,*" answered Schweik, "*but now I'll ask you a riddle, gentlemen. There is a three-storied house with eight windows on each floor. On the roof there are two gables and two chimneys. There are two tenants on each floor. And now, gentlemen, I want you to tell me in what year the house porter's grandmother died?*"

(Jaroslav Hasek, The Good Soldier Schweik)

Valid information reflecting project status can be produced only by integration of quantitative and qualitative data. Decisions can be based only on software measurements and data representing those measurements. Differentiation between the estimated and actual software size does not provide enough information to take action. The size difference may be a result of a number of things: Either the size was poorly estimated from the beginning, or requirements have changed significantly. Therefore, depending on the cause of variance, different actions may be taken.

Issues are not independent of each other. A measurement program established by the organization should never adapt a single-issue focus. When you do issue analysis, develop indicators relevant to the issue. This will help you analyze the status of the project.

There are seven basic steps of qualitative analysis, as shown in Figure 5.12.

1. Measure and collect data.

2. Present metrics.

3. Correlate and cross-reference metrics.

4. Develop indicators.

5. Analyze issues.

6. Prevent problems and improve the process.

7. Retain history of decisions.

This process should be applied repeatedly over the life cycle of software development. Results of each analysis cycle are also fed forward into subsequent cycles.

For a measurements-supported project, analysis of known management concerns and potential problems should be an ongoing activity. New problems, which come and go during the development life cycle should be addressed via metrics analysis. Analysis of known problems can lead to discovery of hidden issues. This methodology provides a predefined measurement infrastructure for applying metrics to a core set of common software project management issues.

There are relationships among those issues. The management of those relationships will allow minimizing the tradeoff between cost/schedule and quality. A focus on quality in the early stages of the life cycle will lead to lower total development costs than could be achieved without that focus.

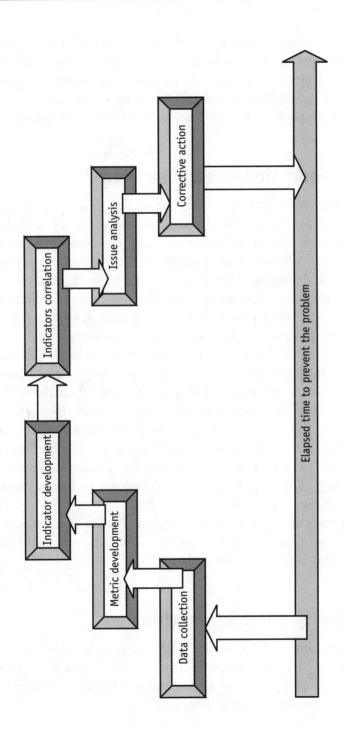

Figure 5.12 Elapsed time to prevent problems.

Resource issues deal with monitoring of resource allocations and the adequacy of planned and actual resources. Progress issues focus on the status of the project and projections of future performance. Technical characteristics/quality issues deal with the quality of the products under development and help to focus attention on critical components.

The goal–question–metric method

In 1988, Vic Basili and H. Dieter Rombach developed the goal–question–metric (GQM) method at the University of Maryland [7]. This method is probably the most effective available for defining and applying metrics for the software process. This method provides a top-down approach to the definition of the metrics, and interpretation of the measured data is done in a bottom-up way. The top-down and bottom-up approach helps software project management and software engineers to share the same perspective about the target of measurements.

The GQM method is based on a process in which the organizational goals desired from the process are defined first. The goals are defined in terms of purpose, perspective, and environment. Then the goals are refined into a set of questions to be answered. The intent here is to quantify the goals. The third step is to identify the metrics that provide information to answer the questions and build matrices to indicate relationships between goals, questions, and metrics. The last step is the most important step. This step is to provide a feedback to the management based on answered questions.

The benefits of the GQM method are very clear. The measurements are implemented for the specific set of goals and have the standard set of rules describing how to interpret the measurement results in the context of specified goals.

The maturity climbing machine

After our brief introduction to the GQM method, let's go back to the maturity curve. To climb a maturity curve, we need some kind of a mental device that can help us climb. Let us apply the GQM method and build some kind of imaginary vehicle (Figure 5.13).

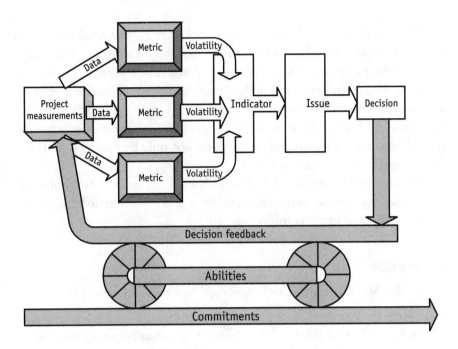

Figure 5.13 The maturity climbing model.

The vehicle should stay firm on the ground of organizational commitments to improve software development processes. Middle management should support senior management and be able to see the forest behind the trees of everyday problems associated with project deliverables.

The following quote illustrates the lack of both commitment to process improvement and senior management support: "We do not have time (8 weeks to alpha) to mandate and implement process changes at this point for this project just to get to Level 2. We just went through the horrendously painful exercise of cutting a bunch of the release out in order to alleviate risk due to an underestimated schedule."

The wheels of our vehicle are made from the developed ability of the organization to implement the software process competently. That includes a buildup of different capabilities including the project estimating procedure. Building organizational abilities means not relying on a subjective and intuitive process influenced by such factors as personality, opinions, and schedule pressure.

The heavy frame of decision feedback carries the load of project activities, represented by management and software metrics. The nature of decisions to be made dictates many of the input parameters for the metrics. Those metrics and indicators should cover the entire software development process and be analyzed to identify potential software development and management problems. The presented information should be communicated and understood not only by management, but by the development staff as well.

The data, which feed metrics, should be a set of quantitative improvement goals that can be compared with the actual results in order to derive a strategy for the process improvement.

References

[1] Minsky, M., *The Society of Mind,* New York: Simon and Schuster, 1988.

[2] Schenk, R., *Conceptual Information Processing,* 1975

[3] Paulk, M. C., et al.,*The Capability Maturity Model: Guidelines for Improving the Software Process,* Reading, MA: Addison-Wesley, 1995.

[4] Klein, L.R., *An Introduction to Econometrics,* Englewood-Cliffs, NJ: Prentice-Hall, 1962.

[5] *Streamlined Integrated Software Metrics Approach Guidebook* (SISMA), U.S. Army CECOM, 1993

[6] Brunner, J. S., *The Process of Education,* Cambridge, MA: Harvard University Press, 1960.

[7] Basili, V. R., and H. D. Dieter,*Tailoring the Software Process to Project Goals and Environment,* Department of Computer Science, University of Maryland, ACM, 1987.

6

Measurements, Attributes, and Data

Measurement

"If you want truth," Nasrudin told a group of Seekers who had come to hear his teachings, "you will have to pay for it."
"But why should you have to pay for something like truth?" asked one of the company.
"Have you not noticed," said Nasrudin, "that it is the scarcity of a thing which determines the value?"

The biggest problem faced by a majority of companies is not the problem of software process improvement or CMM implementation; it is a problem of data collection. We do not really like and do not have resources to collect the project data. Even when the data are collected, we do not know what to do with the collected data. We do not trust the data. Data from past projects are like bad dreams we want to forget and eliminate.

There are number of different reasons why we have this attitude toward data. First, measurements, especially in the software project management field, are badly misunderstood. It is easy to understand the measurements we use in our everyday life: length, height, weight, and volume. They are natural and are used all the time. On the contrary, to understand and accept the fact that measurements of such software project parameters as complexity, design progress, or number of lines of code involve the same kind of thinking and procedures is much harder to do.

Another reason we are hesitant about taking measurements is that we cannot accept the fact that we can measure anything possible if we set up some reasonable rules. The third reason is that we do not accept the need to establish a set of rules, which can be verified, tested, adjusted, and adapted as procedures.

There are two definitions of measurement. The first definition comes from N. Campbell's book, *What Is Science?* His definition of measurement is "the assignment of numbers to represent properties" [1]. The second definition comes from S. Stevens: "In the broadest sense, measurement is the assignment of numerals to objects or events according to rules" [2]. Those two definitions do not say anything about the quality of the rules or the procedures. What they say has been summarized by F. Kerlinger, who taught organizational behavior at New York University: "Measurement is a game we play with objects and numerals. Games have rules. It is of course important for other reasons that the rules be 'good' rules, but whether the rules are 'good' or 'bad,' the procedure is still measurement" [3].

A numeral does not have a quantitative meaning and it remains a mere symbol unless we assign such meaning, like assigning numbers to football players. When we appoint the quantitative meaning to a numeral, it becomes a number.

Rules play the most important role in the measurement process. Rules provide guidance; they provide a method for how to proceed. Let us look at the example of measuring cyclomatic complexity. Complexity measures provide quantitative information about the internal structure of software modules. If the complexity rating is low, it is easier to test and maintain the software, which results in fewer customer complaints and reduced costs.

In the following example, we look at McCabe's cyclomatic complexity measure. In this example, the measurement rule says: "Assign the numerals from 1 and higher to the software modules according to the cyclomatic complexity of the modules." If a module is not complex, appoint numbers from 1 to 10, and so forth. The function for the calculation of the cyclomatic complexity is: *Cyclomatic Complexity* $= E - N + 2P$, where E is the number of edges (program flows between nodes), N is the number of nodes (groups in sequential program statements), and P is the number of connected components. Here, the cyclomatic complexity is a rule, a rule of correspondence. This rule assigns to each measured module a complexity number. (The cyclomatic complexity of the structure presented in Figure 6.1 is 6, and the rule of measurement is the specified algorithm.)

"Any measurement procedure, then, sets up a set of ordered pairs, the first member of each pair being the object measured, and the second

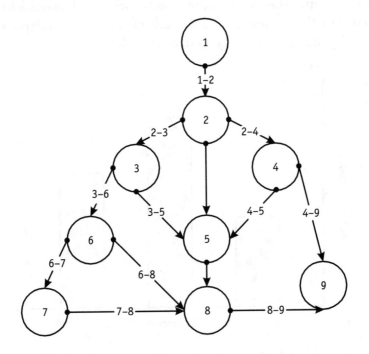

Figure 6.1 Cyclomatic complexity.

member the numeral assigned to the object according to the measurement rule, whatever it is. We can thus write a general equation for any measurement procedure:

$$f = \{(x, y); x = any\ object,\ and\ y = a\ numeral\}.$$

"This is read: 'The function, f, or the rule of correspondence, is equal to the set of ordered pairs (x, y) such that x is an object and each corresponding y is a numeral.' This is a general rule and will fit any case of measurement" [3].

Let's look at another example using cyclomatic complexity to illustrate Kerlinger's statement (Figure 6.2). The modules to be measured, the x's, are 100 software modules. The numerals are the ranges of the cyclomatic complexity. Let us assume that the rule is as follows: "If the software modules have low complexity, give them a range from 0 to 25. If the software modules have medium complexity, give them a range from 25 to 75. The high complexity modules are assigned ranges from 75 and up." This simply means that the set of 100 modules has to be divided into three subsets, and to each of them the numeral will be assigned by the mean of f – cyclomatic complexity.

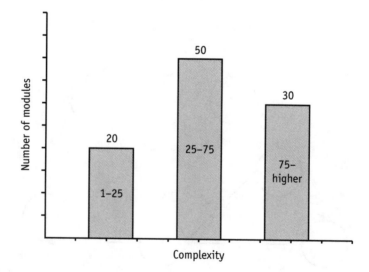

Figure 6.2   The complexity metric.

The practical benefit of the last example is very clear. The lower complexity rating reflects software that is easy to test and maintain. The presented information helps not only to identify the modules with high complexity (the first example), but to make clear the bigger picture (second example), from the management decision-making perspective, in terms of the resources available to test the software.

Always define rules before measuring. Measurements should reflect reality.

Process attributes and data

It is very important to realize that the data we collect will be used for correlation, interpretation, and improvement of the software development process. So before you start collecting any data, you have to come to an agreement about what core attributes will be used to provide project management and software developers with needed information.

Core attributes represent the set of criteria needed to assess project implementation process and risk. The core attributes should be independent from project environment and implementation details. A good example of core attributes is given by NASA's Software Assurance Technology Center (SATC) [4]. The core attributes used by SATC were defined as shown in Table 6.1 and can be applied to any project.

The attributes should be quantified. That is where the core metrics come into play. SATC defines the core metrics as shown in Table 6.2.

Each metric, by itself, represents a small piece of information and can be applicable to more than one attribute, but when joined together, the metrics represent a process that you can control and manage. *Do not define metrics unless you know how the metric information is going to be used.*

Four dimensions of data collection

Let's take a look at a structure for our data collection. We can formulate the model as follows: *Data collection is a process based on measurement activities performed during the product development process to support project management decision making.*

Table 6.1
Core Attributes of SATC

Ambiguity	Multiple interpretations
Completeness	All components contained within
Comprehensiveness	Single test verification per requirement/design feature
Consistency	Agreement of all levels with higher level documents
Correctness	Specifications are fulfilled
Documentation	Description of the content
Efficiency	Availability and usage of resources
Error detection	Rate error located and repaired
Feasibility	Ability to complete with specified resources
Maintainability	Easy to locate and correct faults
Reuse	Ability to apply or use module in a different content
Schedule	Definitions of milestones and their attainability
Structure/architecture	Structure of framework of the module
Testability	Rate of testing and code correction
Volatility	Intensity and distribution of changes
Verifiability	Ability to trace each component from requirement to software to test

Table 6.2
Core Metrics of SATC

Baseline counts	Initial or base number of requirements
Complexity (of design)	Data flow within and between segments
Documentation	Internal or external documenting
Errors/faults/changes	Count, type, criticality, and time to find/fix
Module complexity	Logic, data, and calling within a module
Module size	Line or token count within module
Resources	Personnel hours or effort expended
Structure	Level/depth within document requirement is specified
Terminology	Phraseology of requirements (e.g., use of imperatives, continuances)
Traceability	Requirements traced to design component to code module to test number

Collection of data is performed during software development life-cycle activities such as reviews, meetings, software inspections, and activity outputs including requirements definition or design or code implementation completion. Knowing how the metric is going to be used is very helpful when planning how to collect data.

The duration and rate of change of the activity determine the frequency of data collection. Most of the data are rate driven and collected on a periodic basis, but some data collection is event driven. A good example of event-driven data is the data collected from inspections and reviews.

The interpretation of the metric should be planned: How will the data be used, and how will you respond to the discrepancies discovered? Nobody needs an ad hoc metrification process. This is why you should focus on metric usage.

Without a structured data collection process, the collected data remain just a set of numbers without any particular meaning. Without an organizing structure, process management is just a collection of conflicting practices and situations. *It is difficult to learn from past experience and use the past to predict the future without a structure detailing how to interrelate data and events.*

If we look at a graphical representation of the model, as shown in Figure 6.3, we can identify six stages of the software development life cycle, three types of project management activities, and three product components. Therefore, we have identified 54 cells, helping you to define your measurement activities and, therefore, develop metrics and indicators.

First dimension: project management

- *Project process data:* The development approach for the project; the submission dates for the subsystem; productivity data; types of tools used on a project; historical data on costs, schedules, and quality;

- *Project tracking data:* Effort to isolate and implement changes, actual and estimated costs of the project, estimated schedule and the

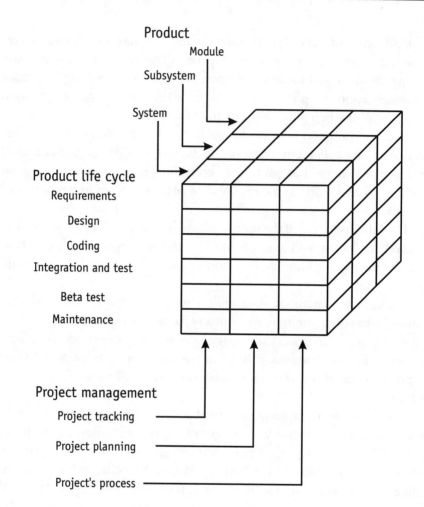

Figure 6.3   The granularity of data collection.

actual dates of project implementation, number of management and technical hours expanded on project, volatility of personnel working on a project, percentage of personnel on a project with needed experience, resources used to correct and implement the change, effort expended on documentation;

- *Project planning data:* Milestone completion, project risks, software estimates, critical computer resource utilization, project effort expanded.

Second dimension: product data

- *Information requirements:* Actual and estimated total SLOC broken down by the components; number of software components completed to date; number of SLOCs written, reused, or integrated; software volatility recorded in configuration management system; number of components changed due to requirements changes; dates when problem is discovered and fixed; source of the faults and category of the faults; total number of changes;

- *Documentation data:* Total number of pages of documentation;

- *Maintenance data:* Total number of hours reported on maintenance effort, actual maintenance costs versus planned costs, number of software components changed due to poor quality or requirements changes.

Third dimension: granularity with which data are applied

This dimension consists of the system level, subsystem level, and the modular level.

Fourth dimension: the time scale

This dimension is concerned with the reporting time interval and whether it is by the software life-cycle phase (at the transition point, for example, from requirements phase to design, or from design to coding) or by event (which is triggered by external occurrences, such as a new item being added to the configuration management system or a newly generated trouble report).

References

[1] Campbell, N., *What Is Science?*, New York: Dover, 1952.

[2] Stevens, S., *Mathematics, Measurements, and Psychophysics*, New York: John Wiley and Sons, 1951.

[3] Kerlinger, F. N., *Foundation of Behavior Research*, Holt, Rinehart and Winston, Inc., 1966.

[4] Rosenberg, L., and L. Hyatt, *Presentation at Second Annual Conference on Software Metrics*, Washington, D.C., June 1996.

7

Software Metrics

To understand how something works, it helps to know how it can fail.

Marvin Minsky

Software metrics are a very powerful tool. The metrification process helps us to understand and visualize the development process as we never have before. The only problem with software metrics is that they represent a social problem because what metrics represent is not exactly what we expect to see. If we see something unexpected, it means that we have to adjust our plans to achieve the specified goal. We do not like doing so because somebody can be proved wrong in his or her assumptions. "We often self-impose assumptions that make our problems more difficult and we can escape from this only by reformulating those problems in the ways that give us more room" [1].

Why do you need software metrics?

You should not use metrics if you do not really know and understand how to apply them, and you will not be able to understand the practical use of metrics until you improve your skill as a project manager. "Nobody and nothing can stand between you and knowledge if you are fit for it; but anybody and anything can stand between you and knowledge if you are not fit for it" [2].

I remember teaching a workshop on software project planning and estimation. My class consisted of two groups of students that had been merged. The first group had already taken the previous workshop on measurements and metrics. The second group decided just to get knowledge about planning and estimation and to ignore the first session. The first group of students was very active during the workshop. They planned what data should be collected for the historical analysis of past projects in order to use them for future project planning and estimation. They built their own metrics set for project control. They were able to apply their knowledge to estimates about their present project. One project manager from the first group made a comment during the class: "Metrics, it is very simple. It's like, duhh, if you really understand how to use and apply it." The second group looked at this person with questions in their eyes, trying to understand what he meant. They were probably thinking, "I do not have time for all of that."

In today's world of management of software engineering, we come across a phenomenon called *imprecision*. Imprecision is associated with the three main outputs of the software development process: costs, schedules, and quality. In different stages of the software development life cycle the degree of imprecision changes. We talk about the same issues differently and, in most cases, as an example, the issue of quality becomes the issue of convenience. (How do we know that software is ready to be shipped to the customer site? In many cases, we are shipping the software not because we are satisfied with the quality of the product, but because we were told to ship.)

We do not really pay any attention to this phenomenon. That is how we manage software projects. We do software project planning, estimate the outcome, and make decisions, but not in quantitative terms. The description of the process of a development software project includes a certain degree of fuzziness:

- "The project is very complex, it might take more development time."

- "We are making a lot of progress."

- "We do not have sufficient resources to complete the project."

- "Let's just cut the requirements!"

Project managers constantly face a wide spectrum of problems. They must cope with a paradigm in which most projects are behind schedule and costs are exceeding budgets. They must decide how to allocate limited financial and personnel resources in order to satisfy their customer's requirements as well as the organization's strategic business plan. Maturing the process of software development continuously requires a source of information representing the effectiveness of process performance and software maturity. Process effectiveness should be measured to ensure that software development is under control. Software maturity is measured to ensure that a software product is ready to be delivered to the end user.

There is substantial confusion among project managers about the exact meaning and quantification of the project data. The measurements taken and data collected represent the knowledge of the project or the process of software development. Metrics are merely the measured data points.

The main purpose of software metrics is to give actual values to the process of moving from a known cause to a related effect. Metrics provide a priori reasoning in software engineering.

Objectively quantifying the quality and reliability of software and translating this information into the corresponding cost/risk and cost/benefit equation at all stages of the software life cycle is an essential issue for the commercial industry and the Department of Defense.

As an example, let's discuss four KPAs of the repeatable level, which set the foundation for achieving a higher maturity level.

1. *Requirements management* means that you put in place a project-wide process for managing and controlling requirements in a predictable and repeatable process. Every product is delivered by a project. A project takes a set of product level requirements and delivers a product that satisfies these requirements. A requirement is a measurable definition of what a product will do. All real projects have to deal with requirements changes. These changes can result from factors external to the project, such as customer and management pressure, or internal to the project, such as requirements analysis that reveals incomplete or inconsistent requirements or requirements that are not technically feasible.

2. *Configuration management* refers to the approval and implementation of all changes. Changes are tracked from the time they are proposed throughout the software life cycle. For example, such items as user requirements documentation and software requirements specifications must be physically managed and controlled. Configuration management is a part of the project and is responsible for the creation, maintenance, and integrity of all the components that go into the making of a product. The procedures, which control changes to the product baseline and also process changes, are the configuration management procedures.

3. *Software project planning* means that project management plans and estimates the project. Estimation is based on historical data gleaned from the projects, and major delivery dates are coordinated with the customer.

4. *Software project tracking and oversight* is a very important activity ensuring that everything goes according to plan. Project risks are identified earlier in the process of software development. The metrification process is established to address and prevent potential problems.

The metrics set should be a result of a continuous measurement process throughout all phases of the software life cycle. The metrics values should identify high-risk issues in software development and maintenance.

Here is an example of the metrification of the requirements management KPA. The metrification involves setting up the process for periodic collection of data so that metrics can be used not only within requirements management (RM) but in software project planning (SPP) and software project tracking and oversight (SPTO) KPAs. The SPTO process describes the intervals and data required to create the metrics that should be collected. The data are then presented in a form that should assist project decision making. This is an example of how the set of metrics, supported by documented procedures, can satisfy many CMM requirements.

Requirements volatility metric

This metric is derived from the records of requirements change control (configuration management system). It indicates stability over time and is presented as a graph of the quantity of requirements changes per specified interval. By using this metric, project managers can identify present and potential problems with the requirements specification and quantify the degree of change.

Breadth of testing metric

This metric is derived from the requirements traceability matrix. It presents the number of requirements that have been tested. It is expressed as either a percentage or total tested. Use of this metric allows the project manager to determine the progress of the project in meeting the project's objective.

Requirements traceability metric

This metric is derived from the requirements traceability matrix. This metric is a simple calculation of the number of highest level requirements traceable to all lower level documents and is expressed as a percentage. Use of this metric allows project managers to determine the progress of the project by reviewing, analyzing, documenting, communicating, and testing the requirements.

Requirements traceability matrix

This matrix is used to trace requirements throughout the project. A requirements traceability matrix is a table of entries that trace each specific requirement throughout the development life cycle to final testing (Table 7.1). It is used as a tool to identify the affected areas when a change to a requirement is proposed, as well as a basis for metrics collection. Each requirement is broken down as it goes through the matrix from left to right.

Collecting data and developing metrics because something is measurable, or just for the purpose of satisfying the requirements of CMM or to keep assessors happy is a waste of time and money. Companies that are religiously involved in process management know that. The metrics process must be an integral part of the overall management process and software engineering infrastructure. There are multiple sources of data, such as knowledge obtained from the analysis of metrics, that are quantitative and objective; there is also knowledge about the project that is subjective or objective and quantitative or qualitative. All of these sources of data form the basis for project assessment and management decision making.

The entire metrification process is driven by current and anticipated project activities. The management information needed defines what data should be collected for the management decision process. By using and correlating the metrics you will be able to find answers because all of the information needed to understand and prevent a potential problem is right there with the statement of the problem.

Table 7.1
Sample Requirements Traceability Matrix

User Require- ments Document	Software Require- ments Specifi- cation	Component SRS	Software Design Document	Software Component	Test Plan	Test Specifi- cation
2	2.1	2.1.1	3.1	xxx.cc	4.1	3.4
—	2.2	2.2.1	3.2	yyy.cc	4.2	3.6
—	—	2.2.2	3.2	zzz.cc	4.3	3.8

Minimum set of metrics recommended by SEI

In 1994, the U.S. Air Force published acquisition policy 93M-017, committing to improved software life-cycle management. This policy specifically talks about the use and implementation of software metrics.

The mandated software metrics cover costs, schedules, and quality. They should be further subdivided to portray the following attributes: size, effort, schedule, software quality, and rework.

The Air Force software metrics policy became a basic first step toward an understanding of what the disciplined process is. Policy 93M-017 does not provide specific metrics to use, but instead gives a handbook with guidelines describing the attributes of those metrics.

In 1994, SEI developed basic measures that describe characteristics of the project that must be planned for and managed. These basic measures can also serve as a basis for improved cost/schedule estimation and for planning future projects (Table 7.2) [3]. The SEI core measures can easily be mapped into the software development life cycle, as shown in Table 7.3.

Let's take a closer look at Tables 7.2 and 7.3. What is common between them?: the measures of the volatility (changes) and the rework.

Volatility

In a previous chapter we talked about the process maturity curve, which is never a straight line. Deviation from the preplanned process maturity

Table 7.2
Characteristics of a Project That Must Be Planned For and Managed

Unit of Measure	Characteristics Addressed
Counts of physical source lines of code	Size, progress, reuse, rework
Counts of staff hours expended	Effort, cost, rework, resource allocation
Calendar dates tied to milestones, reviews and audits, and deliverable products	Schedules
Counts of software problems and defects	Quality, readiness for delivery, improvement trends, rework

Table 7.3
SEI Core Measures Mapped to the Software Life Cycle

Product	Product Size	Effort (person/ month)	Cost (dollars)	Schedule (month)	Defects (count)
Requirements	Number of requirements and change in number	Person Month	Cost	Calendar month	—
Design	Units designed; change in units designed	Person Month	Cost	Calendar month	Defects
Code	New, modified, integrated SLOC; changes in SLOC	Person Month	Cost	Calendar month	Defects
Test	Number of test steps and procedures; changes in test steps	Person Month	Cost	Calendar month	Defects
Delivered system	Delivered SLOC	Person Month	Cost	Calendar month	Defects
Maintenance	Maintained SLOC; changes in SLOC	Person Month	Cost	Calendar month	Defects

curve is caused by changes in a process. Those changes are information based. The information changes are based on changes in the volatile nature and complexity of the software development life cycle.

The process of software development is complex, but not random. Software management, going by a "gut feeling," has long known that the productivity, profitability, and ability of the organization to compete were somehow tied to the repeatability of the development process. Software managers know that ability to deliver product on time and on budget is enhanced by repeatability. Software managers understand that the learning of the process of software development is somehow related to improvements in the performance of their operations, especially when market competition is a dominant factor.

What is an obstacle to process repeatability? The answer is very simple: *volatility of the process,* volatility that should be studied and controlled before it becomes chaos. Any change to the software within any category of the life cycle causes fault/failure incidents, requirements changes, or product enhancements.

In practice, each real fault/failure incident will be reflected by a source code control system data point, even when those incidents are not reported anywhere else within the development environment. Functionally these data points are the source code file "check-in" events. These data points are available from the very start of coding and are present during all phases of the development process. In looking at a source code control system data point as a check-in event, you will find information associated with that data point. Even the most simple source code control systems contain the following information: date of check-in, person responsible, lines of code count, and source of code file name. The technology that summarizes information about the essence of event changes related to the problem is called process *volatility*. During the development process, source code goes through a history of change based on the development process and environment. Reasons for these changes can be categorized as follows: changes to design, changes to requirements, performance enhancements, unit bug fixes, and system bug fixes.

The software volatility metric is based on the idea that the more code that is "touched," the higher the potential for fault/failure incidents. By dynamically collecting and analyzing source code size data, the potential for fault/failure incidents can be measured and predicted according to well-defined mathematical formulas during the development and testing process.

Here is an example. Have you been in a position where you had to count how many trouble reports had been in opened in a day? Didn't you conclude that it is useless information? "LOC change count is often a more objective measure than the defect count itself" [4].

Look at it another way. If you use the rate of change for the software after the unit test, plot cumulative changes (trouble reports and requirements changes) over time for the whole system and for each module independently; also, with trouble reports and severity levels, you will get more useful information. For trouble reports, at the midpoint of the software testing period, or earlier, the slope of this cumulative curve should change rapidly and begin to approach zero as an asymptote. If it does not start doing that by the midpoint, you are in trouble.

The basic assumptions of software volatility are as follows:

- Size data are collected at the source code level primarily for executable lines of code (excluding comment lines and white spaces).

- Data collection is directly attached to the source code through a file system or a source code control system (SCCS) and data collection is automated.

- Each data point represents a quantitative change in a source code size including SLOC, nature of change, and timing data. These data are analyzed to establish fault/failure incident potential (volatility index and change density) and fault/failure incident location, as well as a time and trend analysis of absolute source code change. The dynamic sizing data are broken down into periodic absolute deltas of source code. These periodic absolute deltas are put within a time context that can establish a total historical picture of code volatility.

- Connecting to a source code control system results in the flexibility of retrieving historic sizing data that can be *related to the event points within the development cycle.*

Let us relate the preceding list to the volatility of the process during which a software product is built. We will express process volatility as a function of software size, effort, and personnel. To arrive at this expression, a data matrix composed of cost element densities yielding a normalized index of process volatility is required. The cost elements used are size, effort, and personnel.

Dn	Sn	En	Pn

where the density (Dn) calculations are as follows:

$$Sn = Incremental\ SLOC/Total\ SLOC$$
$$En = Incremental\ Effort/Total$$
$$Pn = Incremental\ Personnel/Total$$

Next, normalize the density of cost element for the process, or each part of the development life cycle, using an exponential function that yields the stability index:

$$SIn = [(e^{\wedge}(-Sn) + e^{\wedge}(-En) + e^{\wedge}(-Pn)]/3$$

The process volatility can be represented as $V = 1 - SI$.

As stability of the process increases, the process volatility decreases. The effectiveness of the development organization does not correlate directly with the number of developers working on a project, but rather with the capability of the organization to keep the volatility of the process under control. Volatility is expensive because all changes are expensive. They jeopardize the quality of the product and planned deliveries. With volatility, management must allocate and reallocate resources for the rework rather than for new work.

Rework

One of the best descriptions of the software rework metrics was given by Walker Royce in his paper on "Pragmatic Quality Metrics for Evolutionary Software Development Models" [5]. This paper presented quality metrics derived from a consistent life-cycle perspective of rework, which can provide useful insights into how to achieve quality more efficiently (within budget and on schedule).

In simple terms, rework is work associated with redoing a product because it was not done right the first time. Rework is often necessary because there are defects in the product; at other times, it is required because of noncompliance with user requirements or specifications.

Rework is typically measured as part of a cost of quality, quality improvement, or process improvement program.

Software change orders (SCOs) are separately compiled for two classes of change or rework. Type 1 changes (errors) are associated with changes due to product specification requirements. Type 2 changes (improvements) are due to cost effectiveness, increased testability, or increased usability. For each type of change the following data should be collected:

- Number of open SCOs;
- Number of closed SCOs;
- Total number of SCOs.

These data correspond to the "errors" and "improvements" statistics in Table 7.4. These data are essentially atomic (i.e., they are used in the calculation of rework statistics). Tracking open versus closed SCOs can provide a good measure of progress.

Table 7.4
Collected Raw Data Definitions

Statistic	Definition	Insight
Total source lines	SLOCt = Total product SLOC	Total effort
Configured source lines	SLOCc = Standalone tested SLOC	Demonstrable progress
Errors	SCOo1 = No.of open type 1 SCOs	Test effectiveness
	SCOc1 = No. of closed type 1 SCOs	Test progress
	SCO1 = No of type 1 SCOs	Reliability
Improvements	SCOo2 = No. of open type 2 SCOs	Value engineering
	SCOc2 = No. of closed type 2 SCOs	Design progress
	SCO2 = No. of type 2 SCOs	
Open rework	B1 = Damaged SLOC due to SCOc1	Fragility
	B2 = Damaged SLOC due to SCOc2	Schedule risks
Closed rework	F1 = SLOC repaired after SCOc1	Maturity
	F2 = SLOC repaired after SCOc2	Changeability
Total rework	R1 = F1 + B1	Design quality
	R2 = F2 + B2	Maintainability

Next, the amount of software (measured in SLOC) damaged and repaired for each type of SCO is collected.

The "open rework" row in Table 7.4 is the sum of the SLOCs damaged due to the two types of SCOs. "Closed rework" is the sum of the SLOCs repaired due to the two types of SCOs.

"Total rework" is the sum of all the software damaged and repaired.

Table 7.5 defines the in-progress indicators. The following three indicators are defined:

1. *Rework ratio (RR):* The rework ratio identifies the current ratio of SLOCs expected to undergo rework prior to maturation to an end product.

2. *Rework backlog (BB):* The rework backlog is the percentage of SLOCs that need to be repaired.

3. *Rework stability (SS):* The rework stability indicator is the difference between the total rework and closed rework. It provides insight into the trends of resolving issues.

Table 7.6 defines the end-product indicators. The following four metrics are defined:

1. *Rework proportions (RE&RS):* RE identifies the percentage of total effort spent on rework. RS is the proportion of the total software size that had to be reworked.

2. *Modularity (Qmod):* Qmod identifies the average SLOCs broken per SCO. This metric provides a measure of the cohesion of the software architecture.

Table 7.5
In-Progress Indicator Definitions

Indicators	Definition	Insight
Rework ratio	$RR = (R1 + R2)/SLOC_c$	Future rework
Rework backlog	$BB = (B1 + B2)/SLOC_c$	Open rework
Rework stability	$SS = (R1 + R2) - (F1 - F2)$	Rework trends

Table 7.6
End-Product Quality Metrics Definitions

Metric	Definition	Insight
Rework proportions	RE = Effort(sco1) + Effort(sco2)/Effort RS = (R1 + R2)total/SLOC(total)	Productivity rework Project efficiency
Modularity	Qmod = (R1 + R2)/SCO1 + SCO2	Rework localization
Changeability	Qc = Effort(sco1) + Effort(sco2)/SCO1 + SCO2	Risk of modification
Maintainability	Qm = RE/RS	Change productivity

3. *Changeability (Qc):* Qc is a measure of the effort per change. This metric provides a measure of the ease with which software can be changed.

4. *Maintainability (Qm):* Qm is a relative measure of the effort to change the software relative to its size. This metric provides a measure of the expected maintainability of the software.

The metric-indicator table

The Mulla's clock was always wrong. "Can't you do something about that clock, Mulla?" someone asked him.
"What?"
"Well, it is never right. Anything would be an improvement on that."
The Mulla hit it with a hammer. It stopped. "You are right, you know," he said, "this is really is an improvement."
"I did not mean literally anything. How can it better now than it was before?"
"Well, you see, before I stopped it, it was never right. Now it is right twice a day, isn't it?"
Moral: It is better to be right sometimes than never to be right at all.

There is a relationship between software metrics and indicators, and the relationship is causal. The causal relationship is described in a very interesting book called *The Fifth Discipline*, written by Dr. Peter Senge of the Sloan School of Management of MIT. In this book, he writes that the essence of system thinking lies in a shift of mind [6]: seeing interrelationships rather than linear cause-effect chains, and seeing processes of change rather than snapshots. Dr. Senge suggests that the practice of system thinking starts with understanding a simple concept called *feedback* that shows how actions can reinforce or balance each other. He writes that systems thinking forms a rich language for describing different patterns of change and interrelationships, which will simplify life by helping us to see the deeper patterns lying behind the events and the details.

I would like to promote the same principles in this book. Let's look at Figure 7.1. This figure shows the relationships between software project management activities, product perceived quality, and a software development process. The decrease in product quality will result in process improvement activities, which will result in improvement of management techniques.

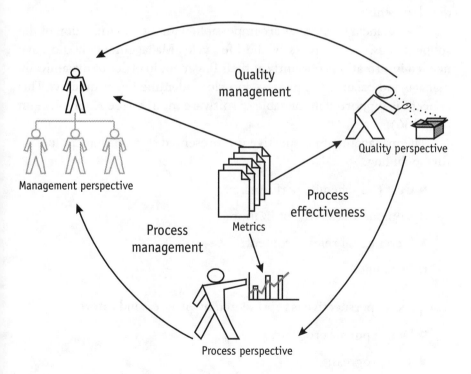

Figure 7.1 Connectivity process and quality.

If we look at Figure 7.1, we will easily recognize the balancing feedback process, which represents the system seeking stability. Dr. Senge suggests that the easiest way to walk through the process is to start at the gap—the discrepancy between what is desired and what exists.

"In our software organization, we spend too much time fixing software bugs and maintaining the product." (In other words, there is a gap between customer-desired quality and a shipped product.) If that's the case, then look at the management actions being taken to close the gap. "We provide necessary training and improve the skill of our personnel, which allows us to reduce bug closure time."

Figure 7.1 shows that a software management process is a balancing process and should always operate to reduce a gap between what is desired and what exists.

A goal such as reducing bug closure time can be replaced or changed, depending on business priorities. Regardless, the balancing process will continue to work in a dynamic environment such as software product development.

The balancing processes are impossible without quantification of the subprocesses, or the parts of the life cycle. Management should have needed information constantly at their fingertips in order to dynamically manage and balance the process and close identified gaps quickly. This concept is supported in the table of software metrics (see Figure 7.2, on page 136).

The management perspective is represented by management indicators including:

- Cost and schedule performance;

- Computer resource utilization;

- Incremental release content;

- Personnel.

The process perspective is represented by progress indicators.

- Development progress;

- Test progress;

- Software growth;
- Productivity;
- Milestone completion;
- In-progress rework.

The quality indicators are:

- Software stability;
- Faults profile;
- End-product quality;
- Software maturity;
- Test readiness.

Those indicators are supported by the nineteen metrics, which follow. They are grouped by three major categories: (1) software management metrics, (2) software development metrics, and (3) software maturity metrics. The pages following present specific metrics and indicators grouped in the table of software metrics (Figure 7.2), and their relation to CMM's KPAs.

References

[1]   Minsky, M., *The Society of Mind,* New York: Simon and Schuster, 1988, p. 144.

[2]   Shah, I., *A Perfumed Scorpion,* Harper &Row, 1982, p. 170.

[3]   Carleton, A. D., et al., "The SEI Core Measures: Background Information and Recommendation for Use and Implementation," *Cross Talk,* May 1994.

[4]   Humphrey, W. S., *Managing the Software Process*, Reading, MA: Addison-Wesley, 1989.

[5]   Royce, W., "Pragmatic Quality Metrics for Evolutionary Software Development Models," *Proceedings of 4th Rome Laboratory Software Quality Workshop,* Alexandria Bay, N.Y.,Aug. 2–6, 1992.

[6]   Senge, P. M.,*The Fifth Discipline: The Art and Practice of the Learning Organization,* New York: Currency Doubleday, 1994.

Software Maturity Metrics

Test rate	Test completeness
Remaining software problems	Average closure time
Total changes and change density	

Software stability
Test readiness
Software maturity

Quality Indicators

Data Collected

Calendar time	SLOC	Number of requests	Number of faults	Number of people	Number of design units	Complexity	Number of test procedures	Cost

Software Development Metrics

Requirements traceability	Requirements stability	Breadth of testing	Depth of testing	Design stability
Faults profile	Complexity	Rework	Volatility	In-progress rework

Progress Indicators

Development progress	Test progress	Software growth	Productivity	Milestone completion

Software Management Metrics

Cost	Schedule
Effort	Fault management

Management Indicators

Cost performance	Computer resource utilization
Personnel	Incremental release content

Figure 7.2 Table of software metrics.

Cost Performance Indicator

Metric Relation	CMM Relation
Requirement stability	Software project tracking and oversight
Development progress	Software project planning
Incremental release content	Software subcontract management
Cost metric	Intergroup coordination
Schedule metric	Quantitative process management
Problem reports	

Data Definition	
1. Cost variance	4. Schedule performance index
2. Schedule variance	5. Estimate at completion
3. Cost performance index	6. Variance of completion

Purpose:

The purpose of the cost performance indicator is to be able to quantify a project's cost and schedule variances, and estimate the cost at completion in order to manage associated risks. Negative variances provide a warning sign that either the planned budget or schedule are unrealistic, or there is a problem impacting the performance of the project. Cost overruns can be predicted earlier to allow time to develop contingency plan.

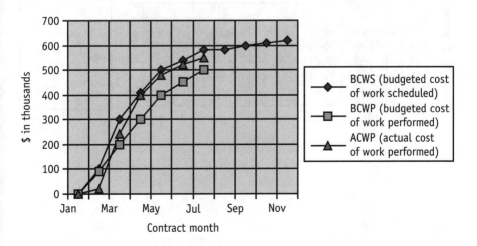

Computer Resource Utilization

Metric Relation	CMM Relation
Personnel metric	Software project tracking and oversight
Development progress	Software project planning
Productivity metric	Software subcontract management
	Integrated software management

Data Definition
1. Average host CPU utilization
2. Planned utilization versus actual
3. Calendar time
4. Peak hours
5. Off-hours

Purpose:
The computer resource utilization metric supports the software development process. The CRU metric monitors three host computer resources: CPU utilization, terminal utilization, and disk utilization. The intent here is to ensure that all required computer resources, which are covered during the project planning process, are tracked.

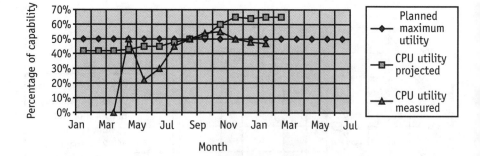

Incremental Release Content Indicator

Metric Relation	CMM Relation
Requirements stability metric	Software project planning
Rework metric	Software project tracking and oversight
Development progress metric	Configuration management
Personnel metric	Intergroup coordination
Faults profile metric	Software product engineering

Data Definition
1. Number of requirements implemented/changed
2. Number of software units designed
3. Number of software units coded
4. Relation of the above to the original plan

Purpose:

The purpose of the incremental release content indicator is to be able to provide to the project manager information about any changes of planned release content. Tracking software development progress is very complex when multiple builds are planned.

The content of each incremental release is of concern because problems in meeting the goals for early releases may indicate problems in delivery of the final release. Monitoring the incremental release content provides early visibility into cases of deferred release contents.

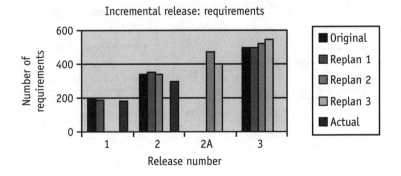

Personnel Indicator

Metric Relation	CMM Relation
Schedule metric	Software project tracking and oversight
Effort metric	Software project planning
Cost metric	Intergroup coordination
Development progress	Integrated software management
Test progress	Quantitative process management
Milestone completion	

Data Definition	
1. Planned staff	2. Actual staff

Purpose:

The purpose of this indicator is to be able to analyze the issues associated with project resources. Review of planned staffing, actual staffing, and staff turnover at all phases of the life cycle provides the project manager with information for resource allocation to resolve potential cost, schedule, and quality problems.

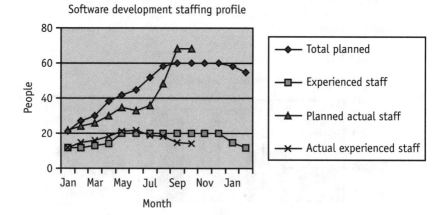

Software development staffing profile

Development Progress Indicator

Metric Relation	CMM Relation
Requirements stability	Software project tracking and oversight
Fault profile	Software project planning
Volatility	Software subcontract management
Rework	Intergroup coordination
Personnel	Software product engineering
	Integrated software management
	Quantitative process management

Data Definition	
1. Cost	4. Schedule
2. Complexity	5. Rework
3. Design stability	

Purpose:

Monitoring development progress once a month during project review is not sufficient to lead to an understanding of the actual risk associated with the project's schedule and quality. The development progress indicator allows us to evaluate the real status of the development effort during the design, coding, and integrated activities. The most important benefits of the development progress indicator are detections of possible deviation from the schedule and indications of significant rework, which lead to the determination of the risk associated with the software development.

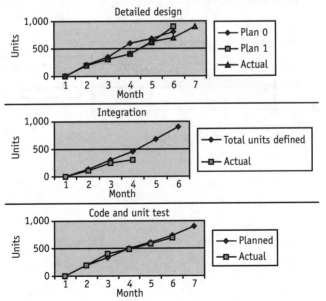

Test Progress Indicator

Metric Relation	CMM Relation
Test progress Fault profile Staffing profile	Software project tracking and oversight Integrated software management Intergroup coordination Software product engineering Quantitative process management Software quality management

Data Definition	
1. Weeks of testing 2. Planned tests	3. Actual tests passed 4. Failed tests

Purpose:

The test progress indicator is concerned with progress during integration and system test phases of software development. The test progress indicator provides visibility into problems encountered during testing activity and reveals whether the testing activity should be extended or concluded according to the planned schedule.

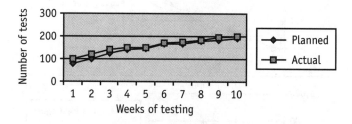

Software Growth Indicator

Metric Relation	CMM Relation
Cost	Software project tracking and oversight
Effort	Configuration management
Design stability	Software product engineering
Schedule	Integrated software management
Staffing profile	Quantitative process management
Requirements stability	

Data Definition	
1. Estimated SLOC	3. Reused
2. New	4. Actual SLOC

Purpose:
The size of software is directly related to the amount of engineering effort necessary to build the software system. Tracking software size provides a source of data for use in size-based cost and schedule estimations. The size of estimated software in SLOCs (software lines of code) is then a target of completion goal, and the amount of code developed to date is a measure of progress toward that goal. Software size estimates are refined, as design is refined. The increase of the estimated size is an indicator of increased effort needed to complete the project.

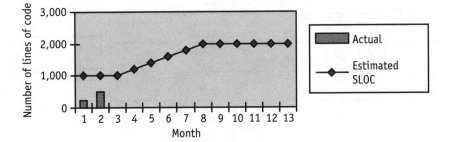

Productivity Indicator

Metric Relation	CMM Relation
Cost	Software project planning
Complexity	Software project tracking and oversight
Schedule	Integrated software management
Staffing profile	Intergroup coordination
Requirements stability	Quantitative process management

Data Definition

1. SLOC/man-hour	3. Actual
2. Dollars/SLOC	4. Estimated

Purpose:

The productivity of the software development team is a very important factor in the successful completion of the project schedule within the allocated budget. Productivity rates are the basis of cost and schedule estimates. Productivity can be expressed as SLOC per man-hour of effort, or dollars per SLOC. The project manager can compare the actual productivity rates to the rate used as a basis for cost and schedule estimates to evaluate the reality of the schedule and budget, as well as to be able to analyze significant changes in productivity rates and take appropriate actions.

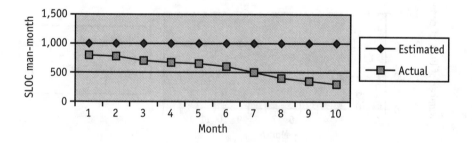

Milestone Completion Metric

Metric Relation	CMM Relation
Development progress Fault profile Requirement stability Schedule	Software project tracking and oversight Software project planning Intergroup coordination Integrated software management Software product engineering Training program Quantitative process management
Data Definition	
1. Planned completion 2. Progress to date	3. Milestone

Purpose:

The milestone completion metric provides information about project progress in achieving the scheduled milestones and completing scheduled activities. This indicator can identify potential problems before they become major schedule slips.

Task Name	Start Date	End Date	June 1998							
			1	2	3	4	5	6	7	8
Task 1	6/2/98	6/8/98								
Task 2	6/5/98	6/16/98								
Task 3	6/3/98	6/15/98								
Task 4	6/2/98	6/12/98								
Task 5	6/3/98	6/15/98								

In-Progress Rework Indicator

Metric Relation	CMM Relation
Software growth	Software project tracking and oversight
Software stability	Intergroup coordination
Requirements stability	Configuration management
Volatility	Software product engineering
	Integrated software management
	Quantitative process management
	Software quality management

Data Definition

1. Damaged SLOC as a result of enhancements
2. Damaged SLOC as a result of modifications
3. SLOC repaired
4. Percentage of SLOC which is need to repair

Purpose:
In-progress rework indicators provide information to the project management about future rework, rework trend, and open rework.

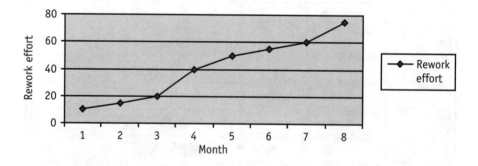

Software Stability Metric

Metric Relation	CMM Relation
Design stability	Software project tracking and oversight
Fault profile	Configuration management
Requirements stability	Requirements management
Development progress	Software product engineering
Complexity	Integrated software management
	Intergroup coordination
	Quantitative process management
	Software quality management
	Defect prevention

Data Definition

1. Requirements added	4. Software units added
2. Requirements modified	5. Software units modified
3. Requirements deleted	6. Software units deleted

Purpose:

During the development life cycle, software goes through a history of change based on the development process and environment. Reasons for these changes can be categorized as follows: changes to requirements, changes to design, performance enhancements, unit bug fixes, system bug fixes, and so forth. The timing of changes makes a great deal of difference in terms of their impact on the project. If there are continuing changes to the requirements or design, the project manager may be faced with a significant amount of rework. The software stability metric provides early visibility of the situation so that appropriate corrective action can be taken.

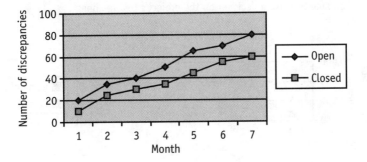

Test Readiness Matrix

Metric Relation	CMM Relation
Related to all specified metrics	Software project tracking and oversight Software product engineering Intergroup coordination Integrated software management Organizational process focus Quantitative process management Software quality management Defect prevention

Data Definition

1. The goal or criteria for the test readiness should be established by the organization.
2. The established goal should be continuously improved.

Complexity	Set the code complexity goal
Requirements traceability	Set the traceability goal
Requirements stability	Set the stability goal before moving to the design phase
Depth of test	Set the goal for coverage
Fault profile	P1s and P2s closed
Design stability	Set the stability goal before moving to the coding phase
Rework	Set the rework goals

Purpose:

The purpose of this matrix is to be able to provide concise information to the project manager about the state of the project, so the project manager will be able to make a decision on the project's test readiness.

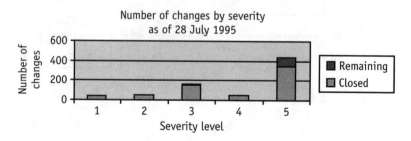

Software Maturity Metric

Metric Relation	CMM Relation
Development and correlation software metrics will help you to achieve the software maturity.	The increase of the software and process maturity is a main goal of the CMM.

Purpose:

Software maturity is a simple evaluation to conduct and interpret, yet the information is extremely useful for developers, acquirers, and operational testers. The trend charts must be interpreted together, as a whole, in the context of external factors such as program schedule and requirements stability. Therefore, the maturity evaluator must have in-depth knowledge of software development and testing.

All trends contribute to maturity

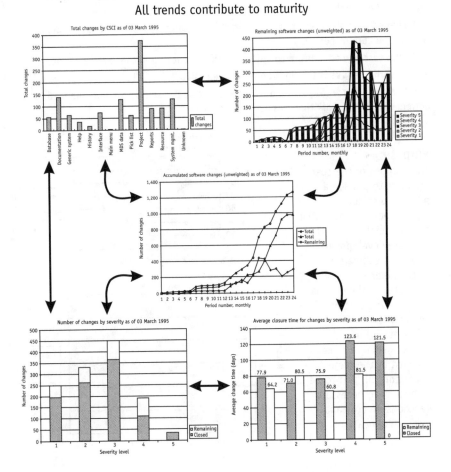

Cost Metric

Metric Relation	CMM Relation
Requirements stability Development progress Fault profile Cost performance Schedule performance	Relates to all KPA required to track the project cost and the CMM implementation, for example: Software project tracking and oversight Software project planning Software subcontract management Software quality assurance Software configuration management

Data Definition

1. Budgeted cost of work scheduled (BCWS) is an initial cost estimate of software project to be completed.

2. Budgeted cost of work performed (BCWP) is the original estimated cost to complete work in the current period.

3. Actual cost of work performed (ACWP) is the actual cost within a time period.

4. Cost variance (CV) is the difference between CV=BCWP-ACWP.

5. Schedule variance (SV) is the difference between the amount of work planned to be performed and the work that was actually completed.

Purpose:

The purpose of the cost metric is to provide a picture to project management of the actual cost associated with the software development tasks and compare it to the planned cost estimates or the original budget. The cost metric is an important source of information for any project manager to keep the cost of the project under control, and to be able to make necessary decisions on cost and resource allocation.

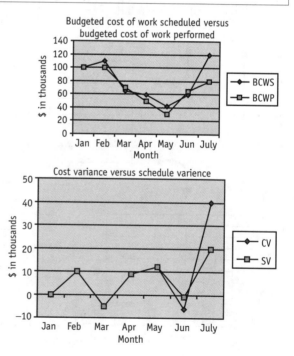

Budgeted cost of work scheduled versus budgeted cost of work performed

Cost variance versus schedule varience

Faults Profile Metric

Metric Relation	CMM Relation
Requirements stability	Software project tracking and oversight
Design stability	Software project planning
Fault management	Integrated software management
Development progress	Software product engineering
Complexity	Quantitative process management
	Software quality management
	Defect prevention

Data Definition

1. Cumulative number of faults detected
2. Cumulative number of faults corrected
3. New faults

Purpose:

Every software development project should track changes to the requirements and design, as well as problems associated with the development process. The amount of faults is not only a quality measure, but also a measure of the amount of work to be done in order to complete the project. Fault discovered during integration and system testing indicate the reliability of software. Progress in correction of faults shows the improvements in the quality of software.

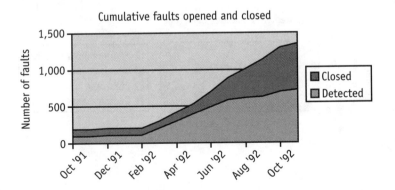

Cumulative faults opened and closed

Requirements Stability Metric

Metric Relation	CMM Relation
Requirements traceability	Software project tracking and oversight
Cost/schedule	Software project planning
Design stability	Requirements management
Breadth of testing	Intergroup coordination
	Software product engineering
	Integrated software management

Data Definition

1. Total number of system requirements
2. Number of requirements added
3. Number of requirements modified
4. Number of requirements deleted

5. Percentage of requirements added
6. Percentage of requirements modified
7. Percentage of requirements deleted

Purpose:

The requirements stability metric represents the level of change in the approved software requirements baseline and identifies the impact of those changes on the integration and development effort. This metric also allows a project manager to determine the cause and source of requirement changes. It is highly advisable to have a configuration management system and a corrective action system in order to derive the data for this metric.

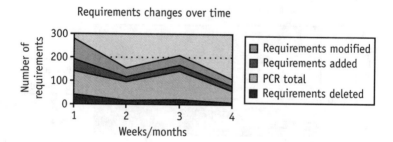

Requirements changes over time

Rework Metric

Metric Relation	CMM Relation
Cost/schedule	Software project tracking and oversight
End product quality	Integrated software management
Test readiness	Intergroup coordination
Software size	Quantitative process management
Effort metric	Software quality management
	Defect prevention

Data Definition

1. Software change orders are separately compiled for two classes of change/rework (Type 1 and Type 2).

2. Type 1 changes (errors) are associated with changes due to product specification requirements.

3. Type 2 (improvements) are due to "cost effectiveness, increased testability, increased usability." For each type of change the following data should be collected:

   Number of open software change orders (SCO);

   Number of closed SCO;

   Total number of SCO.

4. "Open rework" is the sum of the SLOC repaired due to the two types of SCOs.

5. "Total rework" is the sum of all the software damaged and repaired.

Purpose:
Rework is work associated with redoing a product because it was not done right the first time. Many times the cause is due to a defect in the product, other times it is do to noncompliance with requirements or specifications. Rework is typically measured as part of a cost of quality, quality improvement, or process improvement program.

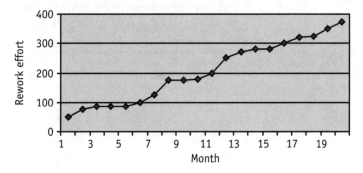

Volatility Metric

Metric Relation	CMM Relation
Rework Software stability Software growth Cost/schedule Requirements stability	The volatility metric relates to all key process areas of CMM.

Data Definition
1. Incremental number of changes 2. Total number of changes

Purpose:

The volatility metric provides a valuable information about the volatility (stability) of the software development process. As the stability of the process or the subprocess increases, volatility of the process decreases. This metric is applicable to all attributes of the process and can be used for the volatility analysis of all parts of the development life cycle, from requirements analysis to software integration and test. Using this metric, you can review the deviation from the maturity curve, as described in Chapter 5.

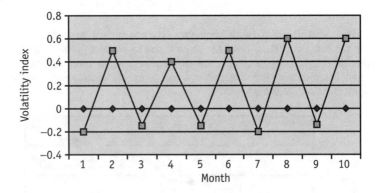

Remaining Software Problems Metric

Metric Relation	CMM Relation
Fault profile	Software project tracking and oversight
Number of faults	Integrated software management
Schedule	Intergroup coordination
Effort	Software product engineering
Test progress	Quantitative process management
	Software quality management
	Defect prevention

Data Definition
1. Number of faults
2. Severity levels

Purpose:
The purpose of this metric to show the overall backlog trend as well as each severity level contribution to the total backlog.

Remaining software problems (unweighted) as of Dec. 25, 1995

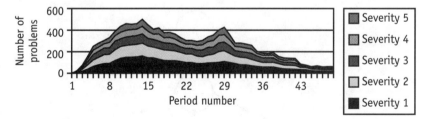

Complexity Metric

Metric Relation	CMM Relation
Cost/schedule	Software configuration management
Test rate	Software product engineering
Fault profile	Integrated software management
Test readiness	Organizational process focus
Depth of testing	Quantitative process management

Data Definition
1. Cyclomatic complexity: $C = E - N + 2P$
2. E = number of edges (program flows between nodes)
3. N = number of nodes (groups of sequential statements)
4. P = number of connected components

Purpose:

The complexity metric gives an indication of the structure of software. This metric provides a mean to measure, quantify, and evaluate the structure of software modules. It also indicates the degree of unit testing that needs to be performed. Lower complexity rating reflects software that is easier to test and maintain, which means fewer errors and lower life cycle cost. McCabe's cyclomatic complexity metric measures the internal structure of the software.

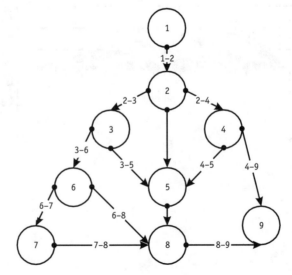

Fault Management Metric

Metric Relation	CMM Relation
Cost/schedule	Software project tracking and oversight
Requirements stability	Integrated software management
Requirements traceability	Software product engineering
Breadth of testing	Quantitative process management
Depth of testing	Software quality management
	Defect prevention

Data Definition	
1. Cumulative number of faults detected	4. Average of closed faults
2. Cumulative number of faults closed	5. Average age of all faults
3. Average of open faults	

Purpose:

The purpose of the fault management metric is to provide a summary of collected software problems or change report data. This metric provides insight into the number and type of problems in the current software baseline, as well as the ability of the organization to fix known faults.

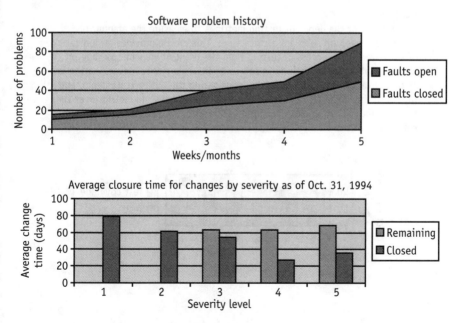

Depth of Testing Metric

Metric Relation	CMM Relation
Cost/schedule	Software project tracking and oversight
Design stability	Configuration management
Fault profiles	Integrated software management
Complexity	Organizational process definition
	Software product engineering

Data Definition

1. The path metric is a number of unique paths in the module that have been executed at least once, divided by the total number of paths in the module.

2. The statement metric is the number of executable statements in the module that have been successfully executed at least once, divided by the total number of executable statements in the module.

3. The domain (input) metric is the number of inputs successfully tested with at least one legal entry and one illegal entry in every field of every input parameter, divided by the total number of inputs in a module.

Purpose:

The purpose of the depth of testing metric is to measure the amount of testing achieved on software architecture. This metric provides an indication of the extent and success of testing from the point of view of coverage of possible paths and conditions within software. This metric focuses on the issue of test coverage and test success by considering the paths, statements, and inputs to the software. The trend of these depth of testing metrics over time provides indications of both the progress of successful testing and the sufficiency of the testing.

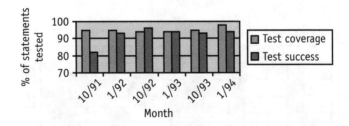

Test Completeness Metric

Metric Relation	CMM Relation
Depth of testing Breadth of testing	Software project tracking and oversight Software product engineering Integrated software management Intergroup coordination Quantitative process management Software quality management
Data Definition	
1. Number of successfully completed 2. Test procedures	3. Total number of test procedures

Purpose:

Project schedules can affect software maturity through test completeness. This measure enables the evaluator to estimate confidence in the software maturity evaluation. A high percentage of successfully completed test procedures, with respect to the total number of test procedures, indicates testing has identified a correspondingly high percentage of problems. One drawback to this measure is that traceability between test procedures and requirements or functions is not part of test completeness, but is necessary to verify the thoroughness of testing. The total number of test procedures typically increases during development and testing.

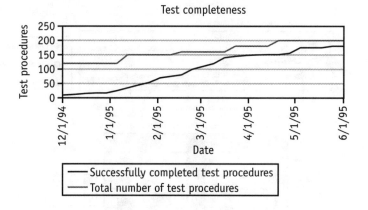

Average Closure Time Metric

Metric Relation	CMM Relation
Fault metric	Software project tracking and oversight
Schedule	Intergroup coordination
Effort	Integrated software management
	Quantitative process management
	Software quality management

Data Definition	
1. Number of faults remaining	3. Severity levels
2. Number of faults closed	4. Average closure time

Purpose:
The purpose of this metric is to show the historical trend to close the software problems.

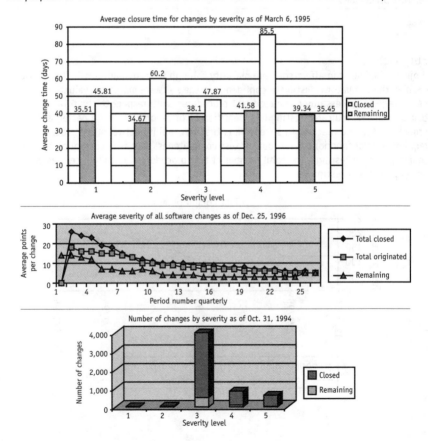

Average closure time for changes by severity as of March 6, 1995

Average severity of all software changes as of Dec. 25, 1996

Number of changes by severity as of Oct. 31, 1994

Design Stability Metric

Metric Relation	CMM Relation
Cost/schedule	Software project tracking and oversight
Requirements traceability	Configuration management
Breadth of testing	Intergroup coordination
Depth of testing	Integrated software management
	Quantitative process management
	Software quality management

Data Definition
1. S (stability) = $[M - (Fa + Fc + Fd)]/M$
2. M = number of modules in current design delivery
3. Fa = number or modules in current delivery that are additions to previous delivery
4. Fc = number of modules in current delivery that include design changes from previous delivery
5. Fd = number of modules in previous delivery that have been deleted
6. DP (design progress ratio) = M/T
7. Total modules projected for the project

Purpose:

The purpose of the design stability metric is to indicate the amount of change being made to the design of the software. This metric consists of two separate measures: the design stability measure and the design progress measure. The design stability measure reports the level of change made to the software design baseline. The design progress measure reports the percentage of the design, which has been completed over time.

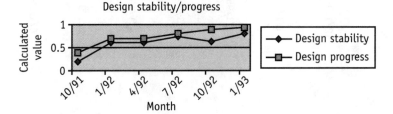

Test Rate Metric

Metric Relation	CMM Relation
Schedule	Software project planning
Effort	Software project tracking and oversight
Traceability matrix	Software product engineering
Faults profile	Intergroup coordination
	Integrated software management
	Quantitative process management

Data Definition	
1. Number of procedures run	3. Calendar time
2. Test rate	

Purpose:

One of the external factors that can affect software maturity is developments test schedule. This aspect can be seen in both test rate and test completeness. An understanding of test rate helps the evaluator determine if software appears mature only because testing has slowed, or explain an unusually high change origination rate resulting from an aggressive test schedule. The test rate should, in fact, affect the slope of the total originated changes curve.

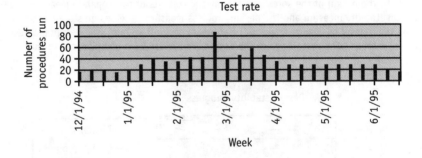

Schedule Metric

Metric Relation	CMM Relation
Requirements stability	Software project tracking and oversight
Development progress	Software project planning
Fault profile	
Cost performance	
Schedule performance	

Data Definition	
1. Planned start date	3. Actual start date
2. Planned end date	4. Actual end date

Purpose:

The purpose of the schedule metric is to report actual project achievements in relation to the original schedule. It measures the degree of completeness of the software development effort and the readiness to proceed to the next stage of software development. The schedule metric focuses on the impact of how early schedule changes will modify future scheduled events. To monitor schedule adjustments it helps to identify risks in achieving future project milestones and software deliverables.

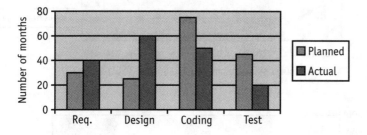

Total Changes and Change Density Metric

Metric Relation	CMM Relation
Software size	Software project tracking and oversight
Software growth	Integrated software management
Number of faults	Software product engineering
Rework	Intergroup coordination
Volatility	Quantitative process management
	Software quality management
	Defect prevention
Data Definition	
1. Number of changes	
2. Change density	

Purpose:

The total number of changes for each software unit helps to identify software maturity problem areas. In addition to sheer numbers of changes, normalizing changes by the size (new or modified lines of code) for each software unit shows which parts of the code have the most change requests and are most likely to require future effort. We call this normalized measure *change density*.

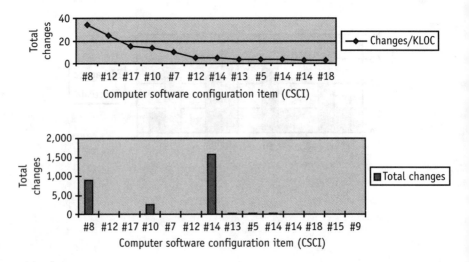

Breadth of Testing Metric

Metric Relation	CMM Relation
Requirements traceability	Requirements management
Requirements stability	Software project tracking and oversight
Design stability	Integrated software management
Fault profiles	Quantitative process management
	Software quality management

Data Definition

1. Test identification
2. Type of functional requirements that are tested
3. Total number of functional requirements allocated
4. Number of requirements tested with all planned test cases
5. Number of requirements successfully tested

Purpose:

The purpose of the breadth of testing metric is to measure the amount of testing performed on documented software functional requirements. The breadth of testing metric can be used to compute three different measures of functional test progress.

1. Test coverage (the percentage of the approved software requirements baseline that has been tested);
2. Test success (the percentage of functional tests that passed);
3. Overall success (the percentage of the approved software requirements baseline that passed testing).

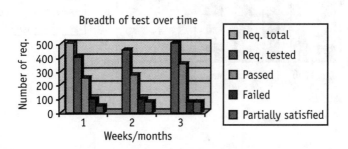

Effort Metric

Metric Relation	CMM Relation
Requirements stability	Software project tracking and oversight
Development progress	Software project planning
Fault profile	Integrated software management
Cost performance	Intergroup coordination
Schedule performance	Quantitative process management
Software size	

Data Definition	
1. Planned (estimated) effort	3. Actual project (related) effort
2. Actual effort	

Purpose:
The purpose of the effort metric is to provide project management with information about the actual effort associated with the product development and to compare the estimated effort to the actual. The effort metric is an important source of information for future project planning and estimation.

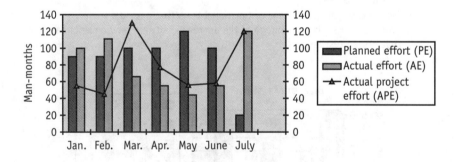

Requirements Traceability Metric

Metric Relation	CMM Relation
Requirements stability	Software project tracking and oversight
Design stability	Requirements management
Fault profile	Configuration management
Breadth of testing	Quantitative process management
Depth of testing	
Requirements traceability matrix	

Data Definition
1. Requirements traceability matrix
2. Number of requirements traceable to different levels of documentation
3. Total number of requirements in high level documentation

Purpose:

The ability of the requirements traceability metric to provide information about the extent requirements to the project management has been successfully traced from one level of documentation to another. It indicates the areas of software requirements that have not been properly defined. The criteria should be established for the requirements threshold for proceeding from one development activity to next.

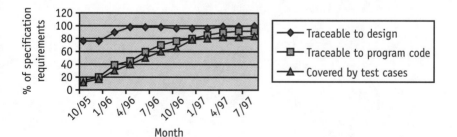

8

A Case Study Evaluating
Software Maturity

Introduction

Prior to purchasing software systems, the customer operationally tests them to ensure that they meet the specified needs. The customer requires software to be mature before beginning lengthy, expensive tests.

Software maturity is a measure of the software's progress toward meeting documented user requirements. The customer uses software problem, change, and failure tracking data to evaluate when software has sufficiently met requirements and to fix identified problems. The concept and evaluation are simple, but rarely considered by developers.

There are three distinct goals to evaluate software maturity.

1. *Test readiness:* Reduce cost of testing immature systems.

2. *Readiness for fielding:* Determine how far the software has progressed toward satisfying user needs.

3. *Identify software maturity drivers:* Identify portions of the software system that currently generate the most changes and may, therefore, be expected to generate the largest future maintenance effort. Where possible, this information should be used to improve the software prior to fielding.

Evaluation background

Software maturity data and collection

The evaluation begins with the software maturity database. The required data are always collected by development organizations. Collection and analysis of the data typically begin when the software is placed under formal configuration control and continue through fielding of the software. The minimum amount of data required to evaluate software maturity is shown in the following list:

- Software change (problem) number;
- Description;
- Software subsystem identifier;
- Severity level;
- Date change opened (or problem found);
- Date change (or problem) closed and implemented.

During development and initial testing, developers and acquirers work together to assign a severity level rating to each problem. The standard five-point scale is shown in Table 8.1.

Severity level categorization

The customer insists that no system can progress to the operational testing phase with unsolved severity level 1 or 2 software problems. According to these definitions, severity level 1 and 2 problems imply the system

Table 8.1
Software Problem Severity Levels (MIL Standard 498)

Severity Level	Description
1	Mission fails or jeopardizes safety
2	Mission degraded with no possible work-around
3	Mission degraded but a work-around solution is known
4	Operator inconvenience or annoyance
5	Any other change

does not meet user needs and therefore operational testing would be a waste of time and money.

Weighting of severity levels

To help estimate the operational impact of each change, we assign a weight to each severity level (Table 8.2). The description of the trend charts will show how these weightings can help to distinguish between many insignificant problems and many important problems.

Evaluation indenture level

While software maturity can be evaluated at the system software level, it is also beneficial to look at maturity from lower indenture levels.

Table 8.2
Weighting Factors

Severity Level	Weight (Change Points)
1	30
2	15
3	5
4	2
5	1

Selection of the appropriate evaluation indenture level is based on software size, number of changes, and the length of time the software change data were collected. As a general rule, we suggest that software maturity be evaluated at least to the subsystem level.

The results help to determine which components or configuration items are causing maturity problems. This specific information helps the acquiring organization and the developer to more effectively address problems.

Synthesis of many trends

Software maturity is not a single trend or evaluation. It is a synthesis of many trends that must be considered together with the external factors that influence them (Figure 8.1).

The case study presented in this chapter is a time-phased example of software maturity evaluation. This particular project was selected because its initial immaturity presents a convincing case for delaying operational use of software until maturity.

Initial evaluation (March 1995)

The initial evaluation of software maturity was analyzed and briefed in March 1995. Although the data were available to, and in fact from, the development organization, software maturity was not evaluated except to track open software change requests. The customer understood there were problems in the development, but had no evidence of how severe the problems were or where the problems were located.

Weighted and unweighted software changes

Like most software developments, problems were initially found much more quickly than they were capable of being fixed. Unfortunately, this trend continued up to the point of our initial evaluation. As shown in Figure 8.2, the *total originated* and *total closed* trends diverge except for a push to close changes from weeks 16 through 20. The result is an increasing backlog of software changes. At that time, we had no reason to expect

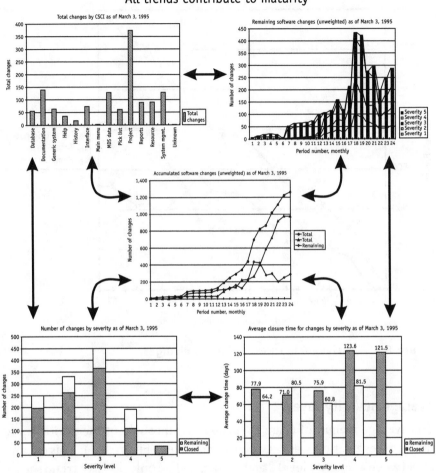

Figure 8.1   Software maturity: a synthesis of many trends.

a slowdown in change origination and current closure rates do not predict improvement.

The unweighted version of this chart (Figure 8.3) looks almost identical. The only difference is that the numbers in this chart represent actual changes and backlog size rather than the change points used in the weighted chart.

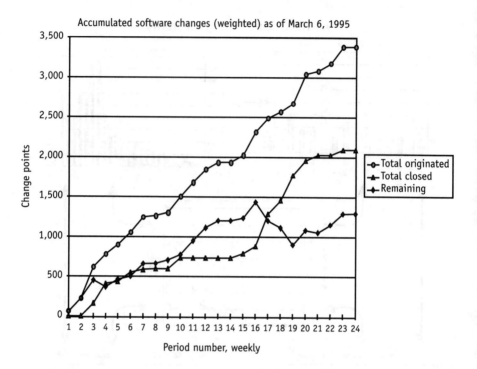

Figure 8.2 Initial evaluation: weighted changes.

Average severity level

The average weight of changes (problems) throughout the period up to the initial evaluation was between six and eight (Figure 8.4). This equates to between a severity level 2 and 3 change. The only positive trend shown by this chart is that the developer has recently been working on the most severe problems.

Distribution of changes by severity level

The distribution of changes across severity levels showed two surprising results (Figure 8.5). First, an unusually large number of severity level 1 changes were opened and remained open. Second, very few severity level 2 changes had been identified. Overall, this chart spurred a discussion of severity level definitions.

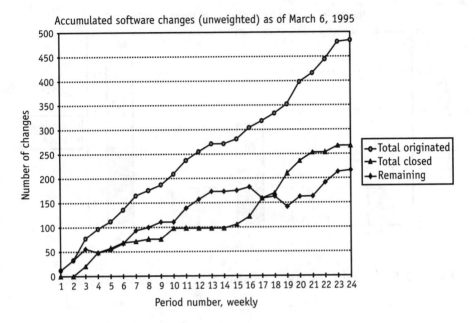

Figure 8.3   Initial evaluation: unweighted changes.

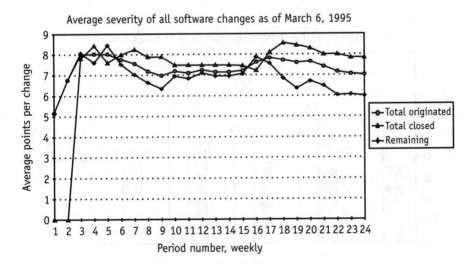

Figure 8.4   Initial evaluation: average severity level.

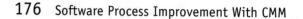

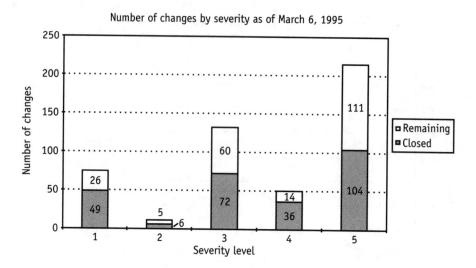

Figure 8.5   Initial evaluation: number of changes by severity level.

Average closure times by severity level

The next set of trends (Figure 8.6) shows that most problems had histori-cally taken between 35 and 40 days to formally close. Unfortunately,

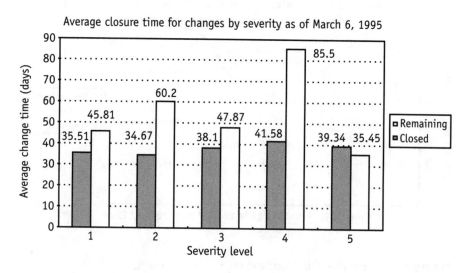

Figure 8.6   Initial evaluation: average closure times.

changes that were currently open at that time had, with the exception of severity level 5, been open longer than the average of those already closed. This indicates that closure times were likely to rise in the future. Because difficulty and severity level are not synonymous, we were careful not to compare closure times across severity level.

Because the maturity data for this development program did not include information about the portions of the code the changes or problems were related to, we were unable to produce change and defect density charts.

Nearly all of the trends pointed to immaturity of the software. In addition, we knew the test schedule was consistently being shortened to save time at the tail end of the development process. All parties agreed to further study these data on a biweekly basis until the test readiness decision in early August 1995.

Test readiness decision evaluation (July 1995)

Between the initial evaluation and the test readiness decision, the developer modified severity levels of many of the problems to reflect a better understanding of the severity level definitions. As a result, software maturity was not as bad a previously thought.

Weighted and unweighted software changes

A great deal of progress was made toward closing the backlog (Figures 8.7, 8.8, and 8.9). Notice that changes in the slope of the curves are more dramatically shown on the weighted chart. For example, between weeks 13 and 17 in Figure 8.9, we see a great deal of progress in closing problems. The trend is more dramatic on the weighted chart because the problems were of high severity levels.

Average severity level

Figure 8.10 shows that the average severity level of recently opened, closed, and remaining changes has decreased.

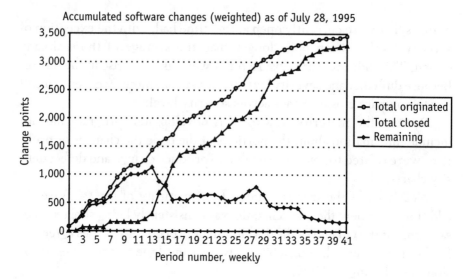

Figure 8.7   Test readiness: weighted software change trends.

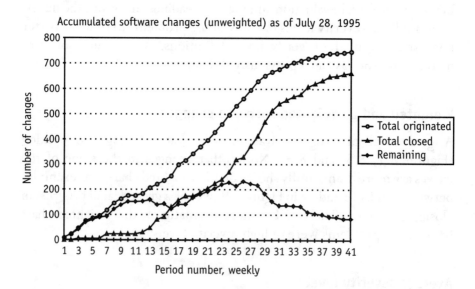

Figure 8.8   Test readiness: unweighted software change trends.

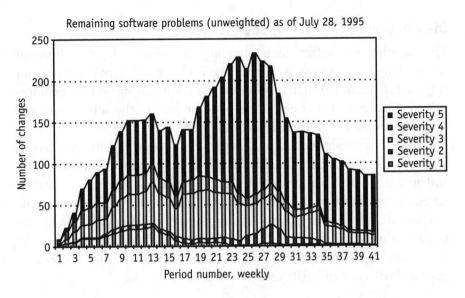

Figure 8.9   Test readiness: remaining software changes.

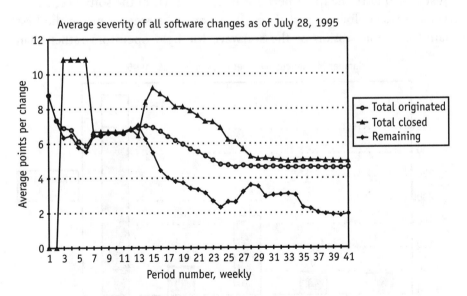

Figure 8.10   Test readiness: average severity level.

Distribution of changes by severity level

The developer's better understanding of severity level definitions resulted in a distribution of changes that is closer to normal expectations (Figure 8.11). Unfortunately, one severity level 1 change remained unresolved. That meant that execution of some part of the software would result in a mission failure or jeopardize safety.

The software showed signs of improving maturity, but local trends were too short to declare the software absolutely mature. For this reason and because of the open severity level 1 problem and the reduced testing schedule, we declared the software not ready for testing. However, due to schedule and funding constraints, the system proceeded to the operational testing phase despite maturity problems. Although this decision did not follow recommendations, we were anxious to see how the results matched with our maturity analyses to date.

Initial operational use (August 1995)

Just days before the first operational test exercise of the software, a new version was delivered and checked out on the system. During the first familiarization session of the software for field operators rather than

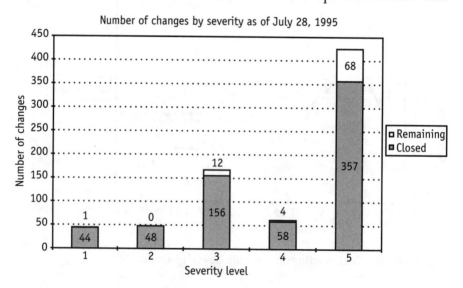

Figure 8.11 Test readiness: change distribution.

system developers, the software worked less than 40% of the time. The list of work-around procedures to software problems grew to more than 100.

Finally, during the first operational use period of the software, it failed dramatically. A software failure caused an incomplete safety notification to system users. The system allowed the users to bypass the warning and overheat some sensitive electronic equipment. As a result, the one-of-a-kind system was out of commission for two months, $1.5 million in hardware repairs was required, a new version of software had to be produced and tested, and expensive test time was lost until October 1995.

Extended operational testing (October 1995)

After a lengthy delay, the system was once again accepted for testing. Largely due to this delay, the software maturity charts appeared mature. Fortunately, this time, the operational testing was run to completion. Unfortunately, the system had performance problems as well as user interface troubles. In fact, users stated they would "prefer to have the old system back." More than 100 software deficiencies were identified during one month of operational use. Six of these software problems were judged to be severity level 1 or 2. Clearly the system, and the software in particular, was not ready for fielding.

Software impact on purchase decision (March 1996)

After a miserable showing during initial operational testing, developers proceeded to fix identified problems prior to the system purchase decision. As a result of preliminary findings, the decision to purchase the system was delayed. The system was to undergo a second round of operational testing to look for improvement.

As shown in Figure 8.12, current trends indicate the software has progressed toward maturity. We must temper this analysis with an understanding that the scope of software testing had been reduced during the period between operational testing and the decision to retest the system. The impact of this reduced testing was a slower rate of identifying new changes. As a result, the developers were able to fix most of the outstanding changes including all of the severity level 1 and 2 changes.

Case study conclusion

Software maturity is a simple evaluation to conduct and interpret, yet the information is extremely useful for developers, acquirers, and operational testers. The trend charts must, however, be interpreted together as a whole and in the context of external factors such as program schedule and requirements stability. As a result, the maturity evaluator must have in-depth knowledge of the software development and testing processes.

Specifying maturity requirements for release and following through with those decisions will help to ensure that time and money are not wasted testing immature software, that users are not disappointed with initial software capabilities, and that software maintainers receive quality products. In the case study, the software maturity evaluation correctly predicted software immaturity. Failure to listen to this advice resulted in millions of dollars in repair expenses and wasted test time.

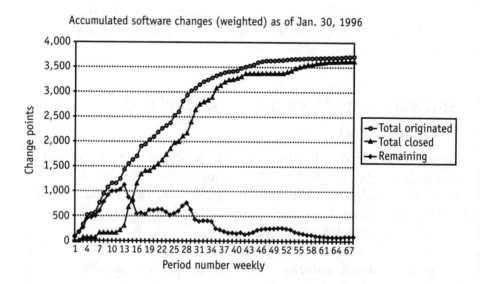

Accumulated software changes (weighted) as of Jan. 30, 1996

Figure 8.12   Current maturity status.

Acknowledgments

The evaluation technique and the material for this chapter was provided by Brian G. Hermann, Capt., USAF, graduate student in Computer Science and Engineering, Arizona State University.

9

Conclusion

This book is not about CMM. This book is about using CMM to your advantage with the guidance of common sense and quantification methods. This book represents a quantitative approach to software management and software process improvement. It does not deny the qualitative side of it. Blending them all together is more important, and the results can be very satisfying.

At one time, with the development of the CMM model, it appeared as if organizations might combine the best from unstructured and structured organizational policies and procedures of all kinds, integrating information from all available sources. Unfortunately, many of the findings of the software capabilities evaluations (SCEs) were disappointing because the majority of organizations could not fit together many pieces of the jigsaw puzzle referred to as "key process areas."

At the same time, while measurements in CMM have to be used in service of the CMM, the model itself does not provide guidance for measurements, and organizations do not recognize the relationship between the CMM and process measurements.

To manage the process, a large quantity of information should be processed. The process life cycle can be filled with many different events. Very often, one piece of information coexists for a long period of time with another piece of information, and the interaction between them generates brand new information.

All software projects are different. Most projects have very comprehensive plans with project milestones, represented by Gantt or Pert charts. Project managers create estimates—mostly with a crystal ball. Unfortunately, they lack a real means of monitoring project status. The estimates contain many inconsistencies from which it is impossible to glean information for making a decision. These projects provide a false sense of security, sometimes supported by the variety of project management tools.

Over many years, I have witnessed quite a few software projects that could be best described as projects of "how to blow the budget and produce poor quality at the same time." Unfortunately, this could be a modern-day slogan for many software projects, in spite of numerous management techniques that were developed even before the Information Age. How much time is wasted simply by tracking down unnecessary and useless information, or by discussing issues without documentation proof or that were already resolved a long time ago?

- What do you discuss at your meetings?

- Why do your developers spend so much time learning things that are not directly related to the project?

- Are you making assumptions that are based on distorted information or no information at all?

- Is there an established practice to share the information between the team members?

- Is the information shared based on assumptions, but not on facts?

One manager of a very large software program tried to convince me that for the last two years the requirements had not been changed. He was very surprised to learn from one of his project leaders that there had been changes at least twice a year.

The problems of the project are always the same: Users change their minds, the design issues still have to be resolved after the design phase, and code will be modified to meet customer expectations.

Often we read the books and articles describing different process improvement techniques and say, "This is not for me," or "I'm in the middle of a project," or "I do not have the needed resources." The problem, however, stays the same. To deal effectively with this problem, we must be willing to acknowledge it. Only by understanding what it is can an organization can respond to the problem appropriately. Organizations must be able not only to see the truth but also to accept the truth. The truth is represented by information about the situation.

Information about the project exists at any time. It is the basis for current decision making, which controls the project activity and actions. The action taken alters the state of the project. The state of the project provides a wealth of information about the project. The key factor is not in information management. The key factor is in managing the process of transformation of information into the software project deliverables (from customer requirements to the software program). The tasks associated with software project implementation are transparent to the process of definition, integration, and information transformation. Many different mistakes are made before project managers realize the information-driven nature of projects and management.

Try to think in terms of the maturity curve. The decision feedback of the maturity climbing machine will help you to correct your course and stay on a curve. You will correct your course and go forward. Using the quantification technique, you will be able to see the situation from the quantitative point of view. It will help you to do "what is right" objectively and minimize the damage from the political "who is right."

Understanding the situation is not enough. You have to know what you are trying to accomplish. If a project has a defined and quantified goal, you can tell exactly when you are off the track and when planned efforts have been diverted. A goal can also provide criteria by which to evaluate the organizational process and the adequacy of each step along the way. What is equally important is the setting of goals that can help us to improve our understanding by calling our attention to different possibilities or potential problems that might otherwise be overlooked.

Having a goal is not enough either. The organization should be able to act on and translate their goals into realities. Someone has said: "Faith is not believing something in spite of the evidence. It is the courage to do something regardless of the consequences."

A neighbor wanted to borrow Nasrudin's donkey. "I'll have to ask his permission," said the Mulla.

"All right, go and ask him."

Nasrudin soon came back from the stable. "I am sorry, he is endowed with prescience, and says that the future does not augur well for your relationship with him," he told the man.

"What does he see in the future then?"

"I asked him. He simply said: 'Long journeys and short meals, sore bones and scuffed knees.'"

About the Author

Joseph Raynus is a principal at InfoDynamics, a consulting company in Lexington, Massachusetts, that provides services in such areas as development of strategic direction for use of information in support of projects and business management; creation of new methodologies for executive control over project and product life-cycle development; implementation of process measurements, procedures, and software management metrics; and CMM implementations.

Mr. Raynus is actively involved in the implementation of software development metrics and helps to identify new ways of integrating them into the software development process and project management tools, as well as CMM structure. He has more than 20 years of leadership experience in information technology products, services, and software process improvement, as well as in all aspects of corporate management, including development of business strategy. Mr. Raynus has provided guidance for product research and development, directed marketing and sales efforts, and customer education.

During his career, Mr. Raynus dealt extensively with the Department of Defense, as well as national and international businesses. He was personally responsible for managing projects in France, Germany, Australia, and Japan. Mr. Raynus is a certified CMM evaluator.

Index

Practical Process Simulation Using Object-Oriented Techniques and C++, José Garrido

Risk Management Processes for Software Engineering Models, Marian Myerson

Secure Electronic Transactions: Introduction and Technical Reference, Larry Loeb

Software Process Improvement With CMM, Joseph Raynus

Software Verification and Validation: A Practitioner's Guide, Steven R. Rakitin

Solving the Year 2000 Crisis, Patrick McDermott

User-Centered Information Design for Improved Software Usability, Pradeep Henry

For further information on these and other Artech House titles, including previously considered out-of-print books now available through our In-Print-Forever® (IPF®) program, contact:

Artech House
685 Canton Street
Norwood, MA 02062
Phone: 781-769-9750
Fax: 781-769-6334
e-mail: artech@artechhouse.com

Artech House
46 Gillingham Street
London SW1V 1AH UK
Phone: +44 (0)171-973-8077
Fax: +44 (0)171-630-0166
e-mail: artech-uk@artechhouse.com

Find us on the World Wide Web at:
www.artechhouse.com